House of Commons
Defence Committee

UK land operations in Iraq 2007

First Report of Session 2007–08

Report, together with formal minutes, oral and written evidence

Ordered by The House of Commons
to be printed 20 November 2007

HC 110
[Incorporating HC 727-i & ii, Session 2006–07]
Published on 3 December 2007
by authority of the House of Commons
London: The Stationery Office Limited

The Defence Committee

The Defence Committee is appointed by the House of Commons to examine the expenditure, administration, and policy of the Ministry of Defence and its associated public bodies.

Current membership

Rt Hon James Arbuthnot MP (*Conservative, North East Hampshire*) (Chairman)
Mr David S Borrow MP (*Labour, South Ribble*)
Mr David Crausby MP (*Labour, Bolton North East*)
Linda Gilroy MP (*Labour, Plymouth Sutton*)
Mr David Hamilton MP (*Labour, Midlothian*)
Mr Mike Hancock MP (*Liberal Democrat, Portsmouth South*)
Mr Dai Havard MP (*Labour, Merthyr Tydfil and Rhymney*)
Mr Adam Holloway MP (*Conservative, Gravesham*)
Mr Bernard Jenkin MP (*Conservative, North Essex*)
Mr Brian Jenkins MP (*Labour, Tamworth*)
Mr Kevan Jones MP (*Labour, Durham North*)
Robert Key MP (*Conservative, Salisbury*)
Willie Rennie MP (*Liberal Democrat, Dunfermline and West Fife*)
John Smith MP (*Labour, Vale of Glamorgan*)

The following Members were also Members of the Committee during the Parliament.

Mr Colin Breed MP (*Liberal Democrat, South East Cornwall*)
Derek Conway MP (*Conservative, Old Bexley and Sidcup*)
Mr Mark Lancaster MP (*Conservative, North East Milton Keynes*)
Mr Desmond Swayne MP (*Conservative, New Forest West*)

Powers

The Committee is one of the departmental select committees, the powers of which are set out in House of Commons Standing Orders, principally in SO No 152. These are available on the Internet via www.parliament.uk.

Publications

The Reports and evidence of the Committee are published by The Stationery Office by Order of the House. All publications of the Committee (including press notices) are on the Internet at: www.parliament.uk/defcom.

Committee staff

The current staff of the Committee are Philippa Helme (Clerk), Eliot Wilson (Second Clerk), Ian Rogers (Audit Adviser), Stephen Jones (Committee Specialist), Richard Dawson (Committee Assistant) and Stewart McIlvenna (Senior Office Clerk).

Contacts

All correspondence should be addressed to the Clerk of the Defence Committee, House of Commons, London SW1A 0AA. The telephone number for general enquiries is 020 7219 5745; the Committee's email address is defcom@parliament.uk. Media inquiries should be addressed to Alex Paterson on 020 7219 1589.

IRAQ GOVERNORATES

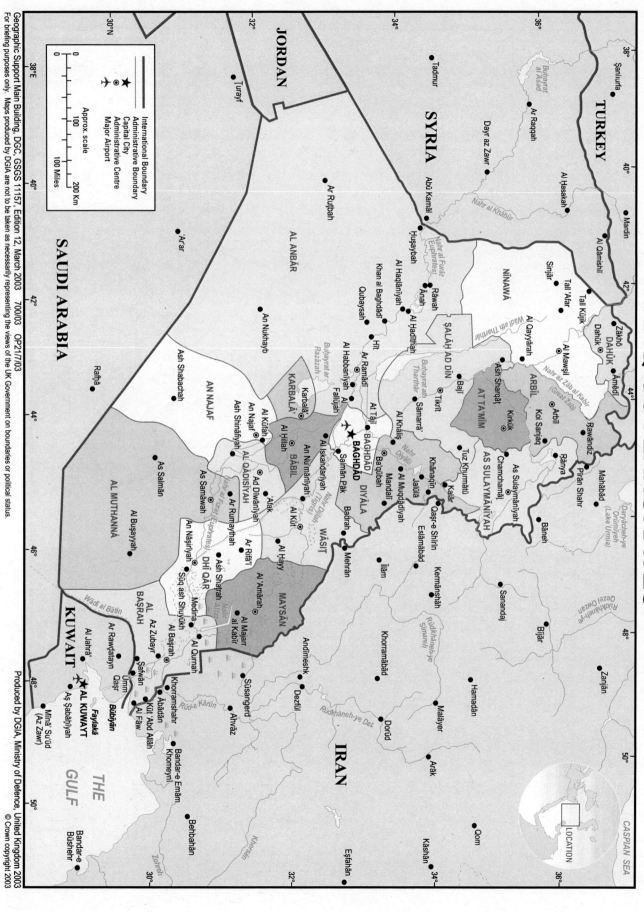

Geographic Support Main Building, DGC, GSGS 11157, Edition 12, March 2003   700/03   OP21/7/03
For briefing purposes only. Maps produced by DGIA are not to be taken as necessarily representing the views of the UK Government on boundaries or political status.

Produced by DGIA, Ministry of Defence, United Kingdom
© Crown copyright 2003

Legend:
International Boundary
Administrative Boundary
★ Capital City
◉ Administrative Centre
✈ Major Airport

Approx. scale
100 Miles
100   200 Km

Countries / Labels

TURKEY
SYRIA
JORDAN
SAUDI ARABIA
IRAN
KUWAIT
THE GULF
CASPIAN SEA

Governorates

NĪNAWĀ
DAHŪK
ARBĪL
AS SULAYMĀNĪYAH
AT TA'MĪM
SALĀH AD DĪN
AL ANBĀR
DIYĀLĀ
BAGHDĀD
KARBALĀ'
BĀBIL
WĀSIT
AN NAJAF
AL QĀDISĪYAH
AL MUTHANNĀ
DHĪ QĀR
MAYSĀN
AL BAŞRAH

Selected place names

Şanliurfa
Mardin
Tadmur
Ar Raqqah
Al Qāmishlī
Dayr az Zawr
Al Ḩasakah
Abū Kamāl
Sinjār
Tall 'Afar
Tall Kūjik
Zākhō
Dahūk
Āmēdī
Al Mawşil
Al Qayyārah
Ash Sharqāt
Kirkūk
Koi Sanjaq
Arbīl
Rawāndiz
Pīrān Shahr
Rānya
Mahābād
Bāneh
Chamchamāl
As Sulaymānīyah
Ḩusaybah
Al Ḩaqlānīyah
Rāwah
'Ānah
Al Ḩadīthah
Khān al Baghdādī
Hīt
Ar Ramādī
Al Habbānīyah
Al Fallūjah
Baʻqūbah
Sāmarrāʼ
Tikrīt
Bājī
Al Khāliş
Al Tājī
Al Iskandarīyah
Ḩillah
An Najaf
Ar Rutbah
Turayf
'Ar'ar
Rafḩā
An Nukhayb
Qubaysah
Ash Shabachah
Ash Shināfīyah
Al Kūfah
Karbalā'
Ad Dīwānīyah
An Nuʻmānīyah
Şalmān Pāk
Al Kūt
Mandalī
Al Muqdādīyah
Jalūlā
Khānaqīn
Qaşr-e Shīrīn
Eslāmābād
Mehrān
Tuz Khūrmātū
Kalār
Kermānshāh
Sanandaj
Bijār
Zanjān
Qom
Kāshān
Arāk
Malāyer
Hamadān
Khorramābād
Dorūd
Īlām
Andīmeshk
Dezfūl
Ahvāz
Susangerd
Bandar-e Emām Khomeynī
Ābādān
Khorramshahr
Bandar-e Būshehr
Behbahān
Eşfahān
As Salmān
Al Busayyah
As Samāwah
'Afak
Ar Rumaythah
An Nāşirīyah
Ash Shatrah
Sūq ash Shuyūkh
Medīna
Ar Rifā'ī
Al Ḩayy
Al 'Amārah
Al Majarr al Kabīr
Al Qurnah
Al Başrah
Az Zubayr
Ar Rawḑatayn
Al Jahrā'
Şafwān
Umm Qaşr
Bubīyān
Faylakā
AL KUWAYT
Aş Şabāḩīyah
Minā Suʻūd (Az Zawr)
Al Fāw
Kūt 'Abd Allāh

Water features

Buhayrat al Asad
Nahr al Khābūr
Nahr al Furāt (Euphrates)
Wadi ath Tharthar
Buhayrat ath Tharthar
Nahr az Zāb al Kabīr (Great Zab)
Nahr Diyālā
Buhayrat ar Razāzah
Nahr al Furāt (Euphrates)
Nahr Dijlah (Tigris)
Shatt al 'Arab
Wadi al Bātin
Rūd-e Kārūn
Rūd-e Kārūn
Rūdkhāneh-ye Sīmareh
Rūdkhāneh-ye Qezel Owzan
Daryācheh-ye Orūmīyeh (Lake Urmia)
Rūdkhāneh-ye Dez
Khorâsân
Zohreh

LOCATION

IRAQ

CASPIAN SEA

LOCATION

TURKEY

SYRIA

IRAN

JORDAN

SAUDI ARABIA

KUWAIT

THE GULF

Qom
Kāshān
Arāk
Malāyer
Dorūd
Eşfahān
Rūdkhāneh-ye Dez
Zanjān
Bījār
Sanandaj
Hamadān
Kermānshāh
Khorramābād
Īlām
Mehrān
Andīmeshk
Dezfūl
Sūsangerd
Ahvāz
Khorramshahr
Bandar-e Emām Khomeynī
Ābādān
Behbahān
Bandar-e Būshehr
Zohreh
Rūd-e Kārūn

Rūdkhāneh-ye Qezel Owzan
Daryācheh-ye Orūmīyeh (Lake Urmia)
Rūdkhāneh-ye Sīmareh
Qaşr-e Shīrīn
Eslāmābād
Mahābād
Pīrān Shahr
Halabja
Bāneh
Rawāndiz
Rānya
As Sulaymānīyah

Mardin
Şanlıurfa
Ar Raqqah
Al Ḩasakah
Dayr az Zawr
Tadmur
Abū Kamāl
Buḩayrat al Asad
Nahr al Khābūr
Ḩuşaybah
Al Qāmishlī
Zākhō
Amēdī
Dahūk
DAHŪK
Tall Kūjik
Tall 'Afar
Sinjār
NINAWĀ
Al Mawşil
Al Qayyārah
Rāwah
Ānah
Al Ḩaqlānīyah
Al Ḩadīthah

Arbīl
ARBĪL
Koi Sanjaq
Kirkūk
AT TA'MĪM
Ash Sharqāt
Tuz Khurmātū
Bajī
Tikrīt
Sāmarrā'
ŞALĀḨ AD DĪN
Buḩayrat ath Tharthār
Wādī ath Tharthār
Hīt

Nahr az Zāb al Kabīr (Great Zab)
Nahr ath Tharthār
Khānaqīn
Al Muqdādīyah
Mandalī
Ba'qūbah
DIYĀLĀ
Badrah
Nahr Dijlah (Tigris)
WĀSIŢ
Al Kūt
'Afak
Ad Dīwānīyah

At Tājī
BAGHDĀD
Al Khāliş
Al Fallūjah
Ar Ramādī
Al Habbānīyah
AL ANBĀR
An Nukhayb
Buḩayrat ar Razāzah
Karbalā'
KARBALĀ'
Al Ḩillah
BĀBIL
An Nu'mānīyah
Al Ḩayy
Ar Rifā'ī
Ar Rumaythah
An Nāşirīyah

An Najaf
AN NAJAF
Ash Shināfīyah
AL QĀDISĪYAH
As Samāwah
An Nāşirīyah
As Salmān
Al Buşayyah
AL MUTHANNĀ
Ash Shabachah
Ar Ruṭbah
'Ar'ar
Rafḩā
Ţurayf

Nahr al Furāt (Euphrates)
Nahr al Furāt (Euphrates)

MAYSĀN
Al Amārah
Al Majarr al Kabīr
Al Qurnah
Medīna
Ash Shaṭrah
Sūq ash Shuyūkh
DHĪ QĀR
Nahr Al 'Izz

AL BAŞRAH
Al Başrah
Az Zubayr
Ar Rawdatayn
MND (SE)
Wādī al Bāţin

Şahwān
Umm Qaşr
Kūt 'Abd Allāh
Al Fāw
Būbiyān
Faylakā
AL KUWAYT
Aş Şabāḩīyah
Al Jahrā'
KUWAIT
Mīnā' Su'ūd (Az Zawr)

38°E 40° 42° 44° 46° 48° 50°
36°N 34° 32° 30°N

Legend

Height in metres above Sea Level

0	
100	
200	
500	
1000	
1500	
2000+	

International Boundary
Division Boundary
Brigade Boundary
★ Capital City
⊙ Administrative Centre
✈ Major Airport

Approx. scale

0   100   200 Km
0   100   200 Miles

Geographic Support Main Building, DGC, GSGS 11157, Edition 12, March 2003   16/05   OP21/1/2005

Produced by DGIA, Ministry of Defence, United Kingdom 2005
© Crown copyright 2005

For briefing purposes only. Maps produced by DGIA are not to be taken as necessarily representing the views of the UK Government on boundaries or political status.

Contents

Summary

For UK Forces serving in Iraq, 2007 has been a very significant year. Responsibility for security across much of South Eastern Iraq has now been transferred to local Iraqi control. Basra, the final province remaining under UK direction, will pass to Iraqi control in December 2007. With transition has come a change in the role of UK Forces, from combat operations to overwatch.

The security situation in Iraq continues to cause concern. While the surge of additional US Forces under the command of General David Petraeus appears to have been successful in countering the worst of the sectarian violence, the precarious security situation continues to impede progress towards political reconciliation. In South Eastern Iraq, there has been a dramatic decrease in the number of attacks against UK and Coalition Forces since the decision was taken to withdraw from Basra Palace, but there has been no corresponding reduction in the number of attacks against the civilian population of Basra.

The development of capable and effective Iraqi Security Forces is fundamental to the long-term security of Iraq and to the drawdown and eventual withdrawal of UK Forces. Significant progress has been achieved over the past year in training, mentoring and equipping the Iraqi Army. The 10th Division, which following transition to Iraqi control in Basra will be responsible for security across South Eastern Iraq, is now reported to be close to achieving full operational readiness. However, similar progress has not been achieved with the Iraqi Police. There remain murderous, corrupt and militia-infiltrated elements within the Police which must be rooted out as a matter of priority. The UK continues to play an important role in training and mentoring the Iraqi Army and Police. It is unclear how its trainers will be supported once UK force levels are reduced further in the Spring.

The deployment of additional Mastiff and Bulldog armoured vehicles has significantly improved the force protection available to our Forces in Iraq. We are reassured that the Urgent Operational Requirement process appears to be delivering much-needed equipment to our Forces in theatre. The planned increase in the number of Merlin and Chinook aircraft should improve helicopter availability when they enter Service and the purchase of additional C-17 large transport aircraft will improve the UK's strategic airlift capability. But current operations are reducing the planned lifespans of equipment and this could lead to potential capability gaps in future. The MoD must say how it plans to address gaps arising from the intensive use of equipment and how this will be funded.

The Prime Minister has said that the Government plans, from the Spring of 2008, to reduce UK Forces in Iraq to 2,500. Important questions remain about the sustainability of a force of this size. If there is still a role for UK Forces in Iraq, those Forces must be capable of doing more than just protecting themselves at Basra Air Station. If the reduction in numbers means they cannot do more than this, the entire UK presence in South Eastern Iraq will be open to question.

1 Introduction

The UK presence in Iraq

1. UK Forces in Iraq are currently deployed under the mandate of the United Nations Security Council Resolution (UNSCR) 1723. This Resolution, adopted in November 2006, provided renewed authority for the Multi-National Force–Iraq (MNF-I) to operate in Iraq until 31 December 2007. A further Resolution will be required to authorise the continued presence of the MNF-I into 2008.

2. The MNF-I, led by the United States, operates in Iraq in six sectors of divisional command: MND (Baghdad); MND (North); MND (West); MND (Centre South); MND (South East); and Logistical Support Area Anaconda.

3. The UK, the second largest troop-contributing nation after the United States, provides the leadership of MND (South East), which covers the southern Iraqi provinces of Basra, Dhi Qar, Maysan and Al Muthanna. Approximately 5,000 UK military personnel are currently serving in Iraq, the vast majority of whom are concentrated in MND(SE). In addition to UK Forces, MND(SE) includes troops from Australia, the Czech Republic, Denmark, Lithuania and Romania. Italian and Japanese Forces, which served alongside UK Forces in MND(SE), were withdrawn from Iraq in 2006. The MNF-I as a whole currently comprises forces from 26 countries. The United States currently contributes around 169,000 personnel to the total of almost 182,000.

Table 1: Troop contributing nations, Multi-National Force–Iraq

Approximate troop contributions (alphabetical order)				
Albania 120 Armenia 46 Australia 870 Azerbaijan 151 Bosnia-Herzegovina 37	Bulgaria 154 Czech Republic 100 El Salvador 280 Estonia 34 Denmark 55	Georgia 2,000 Japan * Kazakhstan 29 Latvia * Lithuania 50 Macedonia 40	Moldova 12 Mongolia 130 Poland 900 Romania 550 Singapore 35 Slovakia *	South Korea 1,200 UK 5,000 Ukraine * USA 169,000

* Numbers not available from unclassified sources.

Source: House of Commons Library [1]

UK force levels

4. At the peak of major combat operations, in Spring 2003, the UK had a total of 46,000 military personnel deployed in Iraq. Force levels were reduced to 18,000 troops following the completion of these operations in May 2003, and to 8,600 the following year. There has since been a series of more modest reductions: force levels were reduced to 8,500 in May 2005, to 7,200 in May 2006, and to 5,500 in May 2007.[2] On 19 July 2007, the Secretary of State for Defence stated that, by the end of the next routine roulement of UK Forces in

---

1   House of Commons Library Standard Note SN/IA/4099, 20 September 2007

2   Defence Factsheet, Operations in Iraq: Facts and Figures, Ministry of Defence website (www.mod.uk)

Iraq, scheduled to take place in late November 2007, overall force levels would be reduced to "around 5,000 troops".[3]

Table 2: UK force levels in Iraq since March 2003

Date	Number of troops
March/April 2003	46,000
May 2003	18,000
May 2004	8,600
May 2005	8,500
May 2006	7,200
May 2007	5,500
November 2007	5,000

Source: Ministry of Defence[4]

5. On 2 October 2007, during his first visit to Iraq as Prime Minister, Gordon Brown announced that UK force levels in Iraq would be reduced to approximately 4,500 by Christmas.[5] The following week, Mr Brown told the House of Commons that he planned to reduce the number of troops serving in Iraq to 2,500 "from the Spring" of 2008.[6] These further reductions, Mr Brown explained, would be dependent upon both the conditions on the ground and the progress of transition to Provincial Iraqi Control and would follow a change in the role of UK Forces from one of combat operations to one of overwatch.[7]

6. During the course of the past year, UK Forces have continued the process of handing over security in the South East of the country to Provincial Iraqi Control (PIC). Responsibility for Al Muthanna and Dhi Qar Provinces was handed over to Iraqi control in July and September 2006 respectively. Responsibility for Maysan Province was transferred to Iraqi control in April 2007 and, on 30 October 2007, the Iraqi Prime Minister, Nouri Al-Maliki, announced that Basra Province, the final province under UK control in South Eastern Iraq, would be transferred to Iraqi control in December 2007.

Our inquiry

7. In this report, we consider recent developments in the political and security situation in Iraq, the prospects for political reconciliation at both the national and the local level, the progress in implementing security sector reform, including the development of the Iraqi Army and Iraqi Police, as well as the impending transition of Basra to Provincial Iraqi Control. The report also examines the changing role of UK Forces in South Eastern Iraq as

---

3   HC Deb, 19 July 2007, cols 31–33 WS

4   Defence Factsheet, Operations in Iraq: Facts and Figures, Ministry of Defence website (www.mod.uk)

5   Ministry of Defence press release, 2 October, 2007

6   HC Deb, 8 October 2007, col 23

7   The meaning of "overwatch" and its implications for UK force levels in Iraq are considered in Chapter 4.

they prepare to handover responsibility for security in the area and assume a position of overwatch. The report examines what overwatch means and whether the force levels proposed by the Government are sufficient to be sustainable.

8. This is our second report into UK operations in Iraq in this Parliament.[8] Our first report, published on 10 August 2006 following our visit to Iraq in June 2006, examined the security situation in South Eastern Iraq and the threat that the escalation of violence had posed to UK Forces.[9] It considered the prospects for transition to Iraqi control in Dhi Qar, Maysan and Basra provinces, none of which had then undergone transition to Provincial Iraqi Control, and the progress in the implementation of security sector reform. We also examined equipment and personnel issues raised with us by UK Forces during our visit to Iraq.

9. As part of our current inquiry, we visited Iraq in July 2007 to see for ourselves the changing operational environment in which UK Forces were working and to meet senior members of the Iraqi Government. In Basra, we met UK Forces at the Contingency Operating Base (COB) at Basra Air Station. We also held meetings with local politicians to discuss the political and security situation in Basra, the influence of Iran, and progress in reconstruction and development. In Baghdad, we met the Iraqi Prime Minister Nouri Al-Maliki and other senior Iraqi politicians and US and UK commanders, including the US Commander of Multi-National Forces in Iraq, General David Petraeus, and the US Ambassador to Iraq, Ryan Crocker. We also visited Kuwait where we held discussions with the Kuwaiti Armed Forces and officials at the Foreign Affairs Ministry and the National Security Bureau.[10]

10. We also held discussions on the situation in Iraq during our visit to the United States in June 2007. We met senior officials at the Pentagon and the State Department, the House and Senate Armed Services Committees and the House Foreign Affairs and Senate Foreign Relations Committees to discuss the security situation, the progress of the US surge of an additional 29,500 US Forces deployed to Iraq between January and June 2007, the prospects for political reconciliation, and the nature and extent of Iranian influence in Iraq.

11. We held three evidence sessions during the course of this inquiry. On 26 June 2007, we took evidence from Dr Ali Ansari, University of St Andrews, Dr Toby Dodge, Queen Mary College, University of London, Dr Eric Herring, University of Bristol, Dr Glen Rangwala, University of Cambridge, Professor Sami Zubaida, Birkbeck College, University of London, and Mr Nadhim Zahawi, YouGov. On 24 July 2007, we took evidence from Rt Hon Bob Ainsworth MP, Minister of State for the Armed Forces, Desmond Bowen, Policy Director, and Brigadier Chris Hughes, Director of Joint Commitments (Military) at the Ministry of Defence (MoD). On 23 October 2007, we took evidence from the Secretary of State for Defence, Rt Hon Des Browne MP, Lieutenant General Peter Wall, Deputy Chief of the Defence Staff (Commitments) and Jon Day, Director General Operational Policy at the MoD. Earlier in the year, on 11 January 2007, we had held a joint evidence session with

---

8   Our predecessor Committee published two reports on Iraq in the last Parliament: Defence Committee, Third Report of Session 2003–04, *Lessons of Iraq*, HC57-I; Defence Committee, Sixth Report of Session 2004–05, *Iraq: An Initial Assessment of Post-Conflict Operations*, HC 65-I. It also visited Iraq in 2003 and 2004.

9   Defence Committee, Thirteenth Report of Session 2005–06, *UK Operations in Iraq*, HC 1241

10   A full list of our meetings in Iraq and Kuwait can be found at Annex 2.

the Foreign Affairs Committee with the then Foreign Secretary, Rt Hon Margaret Beckett MP, and the Defence Secretary, Des Browne, to consider the implications of the US Iraq Study Group Report.[11] We also received written evidence from the Ministry of Defence, Redress, and Dr Eric Herring.[12] We are grateful to all those who have participated in the inquiry.

12. Our report focuses on joint land-based operations in Iraq. It does not deal with maritime operations in Iraqi waters of the Gulf. During our visit to Iraq, we were briefed by Royal Navy personnel at Um Qasr on their role in supporting and training the Iraqi Navy in protecting the oil platforms, vital to the recovery of the Iraqi economy. We also met personnel of all three Services serving in joint land operations. **The fact that this report does not comment on the progress of maritime operations in Iraqi waters is not a reflection of the relative importance we attach to those operations. We acknowledge the important contribution which all three Services are making to the security of the region.**

---

11   Oral evidence taken before the Defence and Foreign Affairs Committees, 11 January 2007, *Iraq*, HC (2006–07) 209-i

12   Ev 41, 43

2 The security situation in Iraq

The political and security situation

13. In December 2006, the US Iraq Study Group (ISG), chaired by former US Secretary of State James Baker and former Congressman Lee Hamilton, reported that the security situation in Iraq was "grave and deteriorating" and that the ability of the United States to influence in Iraq was "diminishing".[13] It said that the situation in Baghdad and several provinces was "dire" and that attacks against US, Coalition and Iraqi Forces were "persistent and growing". It found that violence was "increasing in scope and lethality"; attacks against US Forces averaged 180 a day in October 2006, compared with an average of 70 attacks a day in January 2006; attacks against Iraqi Security Forces were more than double the level of January; and the number of attacks on civilians in October were four times higher than in January and around 3,000 Iraqi civilians were killed every month.[14] Four of Iraq's eighteen provinces—Baghdad, Anbar, Diyala and Salah ad Din in which 40% of Iraq's 26 million population lived—were "highly insecure".[15] Many Iraqis were "embracing sectarian identities". Iraq had become "a base of operations for international terrorism, including al Qaeda". The lack of security, meanwhile, was impeding economic development. The ISG Report found that most countries in the region were "not playing a constructive role in support of Iraq" and that some were "undercutting stability". Iraq, it concluded, was "in the grip of a deadly cycle". If the situation continued to deteriorate "the consequences could be severe" and "a slide towards chaos could trigger the collapse of Iraq's government and a humanitarian catastrophe". In a downbeat assessment of the options facing the United States, it concluded that "there is no path that can guarantee success, but the prospects can be improved".[16]

14. It was in the context of this deteriorating security situation that President George W Bush set out his new strategy in Iraq. On 10 January 2007, he acknowledged that the security situation was "unacceptable", that political reconciliation had not been forthcoming, and that Iraqi Security Forces had proved unable to assume greater responsibility from the United States. He announced a "surge" of US Forces to impose security in Baghdad and the neighbouring Western province of Anbar, a new emphasis on achieving political reconciliation, and new initiatives intended to promote the positive engagement of Iraq's neighbours in stabilising the country.[17] Under the newly appointed US Commander of Multi-National Forces in Iraq (MNF-I), General David Petraeus, an additional 21,500 US Forces would deploy to Iraq over the following five-to-six months to bolster security and clamp down on sectarian violence. This figure was increased to 29,500 following a request by General Petraeus in March 2007. By late July 2007, when the surge

---

13   *The Iraq Study Group Report,* 6 December 2006

14   *Ibid.* p 9

15   *Ibid.,* p 10

16   *Ibid,* Executive Summary

17   "President's Address to the Nation", White House Press Release, 10 January 2007

had reached full operational capability, approximately 169,000 US military personnel were serving in Iraq out of a total Multi-National Force of around 182,000.[18]

15. The US surge in Iraq reached its peak as we began our inquiry. Witnesses to our first evidence session, on 26 June, painted a gloomy picture of the security situation in the country and of the effectiveness of the surge. Dr Glen Rangwala, of Cambridge University, told us that although the surge appeared to have improved the security situation, he was "pessimistic" that this signified a permanent improvement: the surge had led to "a temporary lull in the violence, but not a reduction". According to Dr Rangwala, the number of extra-judicial killings and multiple fatality bombings might have gone down during the Spring of 2007, but insurgent groups were operating outside the capital city, or had just stored their weapons away temporarily, waiting for the US Forces to depart.[19] Similarly, Dr Eric Herring, of Bristol University, suggested that the surge had merely prompted a "displacement of the violence to other parts of Iraq and a destabilisation of places which were relatively quiet". For Dr Herring, there had been "a fundamental decline" in the security situation, despite the surge.[20] Dr Toby Dodge, of Queen Mary College, University of London, suggested that the results of the surge were mixed: the reduction in violence was "incredibly localised and probably temporary". The surge had led directly to the fighters, the militias and insurgents moving out of the capital to Diyala, where violence had increased "massively".[21]

16. According to Dr Dodge, it was the security vacuum in Iraq which underpinned most of the violence; "the cause is the collapse of the Iraqi state". A combination of the brutality of Saddam Hussein, the impact of international sanctions, the 2003 invasion, and the subsequent programme of de-Ba'athification meant that "the state was shaken to pieces" and its "institutional memory" erased which resulted in both a political and security vacuum into which "firstly, stepped criminals, and then insurgents".[22] Throughout Iraq as a whole, there was "a series of different groups fighting different wars" and "what we have is a multi-level conflict" and a "big stew of violence that is the Iraqi civil war as it stands". But despite the different geographical struggles, the common "overarching explanation" for the violence at both the national and the local level was "this security vacuum which these different groups have stepped into, with different objectives".[23]

17. The assessment of the security situation in Iraq offered by our witnesses was reflected in the conclusions of the UK Iraq Commission, an independent cross-party Commission chaired by Lord Ashdown, Baroness Jay and Lord King, whose report was published on 14 July 2007. The Commission, billed as the UK equivalent of the US Iraq Study Group, found that "the security situation in Iraq remains grave and has been for some time". According

---

18   House of Commons Library Standard Note SN/IA/4099, 20 September 2007

19   Q 6

20   *Ibid.*

21   Q 22

22   Q 2

23   Qq 2, 5

to the Commission, there was "currently not one conflict, or one insurgency in Iraq, but several conflicts and insurgencies between different communities and organisations".[24]

18. The MoD, however, insisted that the surge was having a positive effect. In evidence to us, on 24 July, Brigadier Chris Hughes, Director of Joint Commitments (Military) at the MoD, told us that a number of successes had come from the surge:

> The figures for vehicle-borne IEDs [Improvised Explosive Devices] are down; the figures for murders of civilians are significantly down. It is true to say that the additional security that has come in Baghdad has not just been displaced somewhere else; in some of the other provinces AQI [Al Qaeda Iraq], in particular, is being given a hard time.[25]

There were two measures by which the success of the surge would ultimately be judged:

> To what extent the breathing space that the military surge has given in the security situation—and I think it has—has allowed the politics to breathe, and to what extent are the Iraqi Security Forces able to back up what has largely been this Coalition surge. Those are the two questions which remain unanswered as of today.[26]

19. A US National Intelligence Estimate, published in August 2007, presented a mixed picture of the security situation in Iraq. It reported "measurable but uneven improvements in Iraq's security situation since […] January 2007":

> The steep escalation of violence has been checked for now, and overall attack levels across Iraq have fallen during seven of the last nine weeks. Coalition forces, working with Iraqi forces, tribal elements, and some Sunni insurgents, have reduced al-Qa'ida in Iraq's (AQI) capabilities, restricted its freedom of movement, and denied it grassroots support in some areas.[27]

But the security situation was still considered poor:

> The level of overall violence, including attacks on and casualties among civilians, remains high; Iraq's sectarian groups remain unreconciled; AQI retains the ability to conduct high-profile attacks; and to date, Iraqi political leaders remain unable to govern effectively.[28]

The Estimate predicted that if Coalition Forces continued "to conduct robust counterinsurgency operations […] Iraq's security will continue to improve modestly during the next six to 12 months but that levels of insurgent and sectarian violence will remain high".[29]

---

24   *The Iraq Commission Report*, The Foreign Policy Centre and Channel 4, 14 July 2007, p 14

25   Q 151

26   *Ibid.*

27   *Prospects for Iraq's Stability: Some Security Progress but Political Reconciliation Elusive*, National Intelligence Estimate (United States), August 2007, p 1

28   *Ibid.* p 1

29   *Ibid.* p 1

20. On 10 September 2007, General Petraeus reported to the US Congress that "the military objectives of the surge are, in large measure, being met" and that progress in improving the security situation had been "substantial".[30] He stated that the number of security incidents had decreased significantly since the start of the surge offensive operations:

> civilian deaths [...] have also declined considerably, by over 45% Iraq-wide since the height of the sectarian violence in December [2006] [and] [...] by some 70% in Baghdad [...] The number of ethno-sectarian deaths [...] has also declined significantly since the height of sectarian violence [...] by over 55% [...] In Baghdad [...] the number of ethno-sectarian deaths has come down by some 80% since December.[31]

21. General Petraeus acknowledged that trends had not been uniformly positive across Iraq. But in his judgement, "the overall trajectory in Iraq—a steady decline of incidents in the past three months—is still quite significant".[32] Coalition and Iraqi forces, he said, had "dealt significant blows to Al Qaeda Iraq" and had "taken away a number of sanctuaries and gained the initiative in many areas". Moreover, in Anbar Province, West of Baghdad, there had been an indigenous tribal rejection of Al Qaeda Iraq (AQI) which was "maybe the most significant development of the last 8 months". It had helped produce "significant change" in the Province and had since spread to a number of other locations as well.[33]

22. Important as the reduction of violence has been, the surge was never intended to be an end in itself. Its broader aim was to allow politics in Iraq, and political reconciliation in particular, a chance to progress. At the announcement of the surge, in January 2007, President Bush made it clear that the US commitment to Iraq was not open-ended and that, as the security situation was addressed, the Iraqi Government would be expected to secure progress on: de-Baathification, reconstruction and development, the sharing of oil revenues, changes to the constitution and holding local elections. The surge would give the Iraqi Government "the breathing space it needs to make progress in [these] critical areas".[34]

23. Yet, unlike General Petraeus, Ambassador Crocker was able to report comparatively little progress. In what he termed a "sober assessment" of the "enormity of the challenges faced by Iraqis", he warned that progress towards political reconciliation had been slow; "it will be uneven, punctuated by setbacks as well as achievements, and it will require substantial US resolve". The Iraqi Government had not managed to achieve many of the political benchmarks laid down by the United States. However, he insisted that his assessment "should not be a disheartening one", arguing that Iraq's leaders had "the will to tackle the country's pressing problems" and that there had been "more pronounced"

30　Report to Congress on the Situation in Iraq by General David H Petraeus, Commander, Multi-National Forces–Iraq, 10 September 2007, p 3

31　*Ibid.*

32　*Ibid.* p 4

33　*Ibid.* p 1

34　"President's Address to the Nation", White House Press Release, 10 January 2007

political gains at the local level where there was "abundant evidence that the security gains have opened the door for meaningful politics".[35]

24. Ambassador Crocker reported some progress in economic reconstruction and capacity building. Iraqi ministries and provincial councils, for example, had made "substantial progress this year in utilizing Iraq's oil revenue for investment". However, in overall terms, the Iraqi economy, though set to grow by 6% in 2007, was "performing significantly under its potential". Though improving, critical infrastructure such as electricity supplies remained poor.[36]

25. In evidence to us on 23 October 2007, the Secretary of State for Defence told us that there was "a long way to go" with political reconciliation at the national level in Iraq. Reconciliation was "the key to stability" but there had not been as much progress as either the US or the UK would have liked. He concluded that, ultimately, political reconciliation could only be achieved by the Iraqis themselves; "we can only [...] encourage them to go down this road and to continue to explain to them how important it is for sustained peace in their country that they do it".[37]

26. **We note the progress of the US surge in and around Baghdad and welcome the apparent reductions in the level of violence, both against Coalition and Iraqi Forces and the civilian population. But it is important not to overstate the successes of the surge. The level of violence in Iraq is still worryingly high. It remains to be seen whether the improvements in the security situation represent a lasting reduction in insurgent, militia and sectarian violence or whether the violence will once again increase after the US withdraws the surge element of its Forces.**

27. **The Iraqi Government must make the most of the reduction in violence to move the political process forward to achieve meaningful and lasting political reconciliation in Iraq. In the long-term, it is only through reconciliation, both nationally and locally, that Iraq can develop into a secure and stable country.**

The security situation in South Eastern Iraq

28. The situation in South Eastern Iraq, in the UK area of operations, is very different from that in and around Baghdad. In evidence to us, Ministers, MoD officials and academic witnesses agreed that the overall level of violence in South Eastern Iraq was lower than in other parts of the country. The Secretary of State for Defence told us that "in proportionate terms a very small number of the attacks that happen in Iraq happen in the Basra area". Mr Browne stated that "over 80% of the violence is concentrated around a relatively small circumference of the city of Baghdad and Baghdad itself".[38]

---

35   Report to Congress on the Situation in Iraq by Ambassador Ryan C Crocker, US Ambassador to the Republic of Iraq, 10 September 2007, p 3

36   *Ibid.* p 3

37   Oral evidence taken before the Defence Committee on 23 October 2007, *Iraq and Afghanistan,* HC (2006–07) 1091-i, Q 43

38   *Ibid.,* Q 4

29. The sources of violence in South Eastern Iraq are also very different. During our visit to Basra in July 2007 we heard from a number of those we met that the violence in the area was self-limiting since it reflected a competition for money, power and influence between local Shia groups rather than the sectarian nihilism of al-Qaeda; in effect, no party wanted to destroy that over which it wanted to assert control. In South Eastern Iraq, there was no sectarian insurgency and none of the jihadist elements seen elsewhere in the country. Instead, the violence was propagated by Shia gangsterism and Iranian-backed militias. In fact, in the South, religion was seen as a unifying rather than a dividing factor. As the Minister for the Armed Forces told us in evidence on 24 July, the people of South Eastern Iraq were "religiously and ethnically cohesive".[39]

30. Academic witnesses to our inquiry agreed that in South Eastern Iraq the problem was the battle over resources rather than sectarianism. In evidence to us on 26 June 2007, Professor Sami Zubaida argued that "all the sides there are Shi'ite but they are divided along different loyalties to different parties, to different tribes, straightforward gangs and mafias, and so on. In Basra, "the objectives of the insurgency are actually control of material resources: profit".[40] Dr Eric Herring agreed that the violence in South Eastern Iraq was "an intra-Shia political, and effectively mafia, struggle".[41]

31. We began our inquiry in June 2007 at a time of escalating violence in South Eastern Iraq, particularly towards the Coalition, and increasing doubts in the UK about the efficacy of the role assigned to UK Forces in Basra. As attacks against UK Forces increased, some witnesses to our inquiry, and some of those we met in Iraq, suggested that the deterioration of the security situation in Basra had demonstrated that UK and Coalition Forces had outstayed their welcome and had become part of the problem rather than the solution. Some suggested that the UK's military presence in Basra was not only risky but also tactically questionable. And some suggested that military force alone inevitably had a limited usefulness and that a foreign army was an inappropriate tool for the job that needed to be done in Basra.

32. In evidence to us, Dr Herring argued that what was often seen as "the comparative stability in Basra" was not the result of UK and Coalition action. Whatever stability had emerged had come about "precisely because the militias have managed to dominate". This was not stability "in any positive sense" since it represented "a fragile balance between militias".[42] In written evidence to us Dr Herring questioned the role of UK Forces in Iraq arguing that "the UK military presence in Iraq has been tiny and under-resourced" and characterised by "persistent incoherence and lack of integration". He suggested that "in continual fear of being over-run, the priority has been to avoid antagonising excessively existing or rising armed local political actors". Notwithstanding reconstruction, anti-militia and anti-corruption efforts such as Operation Sinbad in late 2006 and early 2007, UK Forces had "tended to be (often uncomprehending) spectators, occasional protagonists and only rarely the centre of power and legitimacy". UK Forces had "engaged in what could

39 Q 112
40 Q 4
41 Q 2
42 Q 21

only be intermittent and intermittently productive operations".[43] The conclusion of the local Basrawi population, he said, was that UK Forces "are making the situation worse and [they] want them to leave".[44]

33. Dr Dodge argued that "there is no stability in Basra".[45] In evidence to us, he stated:

> Periodically, outright conflict breaks out and violence flows. I think to qualify that as low level is simply not the case. People are dying in Basra. Basra is a lawless place where the politics of the gun dominates; that is not low-level violence, that is anarchy, and it could get worse or it could stay at a steady rate.[46]

But despite the fact that Basra was "highly unstable" and "extremely violent", Dr Dodge offered a somewhat more positive assessment of the role UK Forces could still play in the region than that offered by Dr Herring. Although their presence was "limited", he suggested that UK Forces nevertheless were "putting a brake, albeit a rather malfunctioning one, on the swift movement to civil war".[47] According to Dr Dodge, a complete withdrawal of UK Forces "may trigger, may destabilise and increase the violence" in Basra and South Eastern Iraq as a whole.

34. Professor Zubaida called the situation in Basra in June 2007 "desperate". He agreed that UK Forces remained "a brake on much wider violence" but he questioned whether this would make a difference in the long-term. If UK Forces left precipitously violence could well increase, but a withdrawal of UK Forces in two years' time could well have the same effect. For Professor Zubaida, the key question was "what is going to happen in the those two years which is going to lead to a different outcome?".[48] There was a real risk that whenever UK and Coalition Forces withdrew the country could descend into civil war.[49]

35. When we took evidence from the Minister for the Armed Forces on 24 July 2007, he acknowledged "grand scale criminality" was "a huge part of the problem in the South". There were regular attacks on UK Forces at the Provincial Joint Co-ordination Centre (PJCC) at Basra Palace and at the Contingency Operating Base at Basra Air Station. Indeed, as we witnessed, July saw some of the highest numbers of attacks against UK Forces in Basra in 2007, peaking at almost 120 attacks in the week beginning 20 July. By mid-August 2007, UK Forces were suffering the highest sustained level of attacks of the year, an average of over 90 attacks per week over the preceding four week period.[50]

36. Mr Ainsworth, however, said the fact that UK Forces were being targeted was "not surprising". After all, the insurgents and militias understood that "we are the ultimate

---

43 Ev 46

44 Ev 43

45 Q 21

46 Q 49

47 Qq 46, 7

48 Qq 47, 48

49 Q 7

50 See Table 3 below. Also HC (2006–07) 1091-i, Ev 19, Figure 1

guarantor of any chance of progress" and "we [...] are effectively providing the backbone of stability" in South Eastern Iraq.[51]

37. Since July 2007, the security situation in Basra has changed significantly. The handover of Basra Palace to Iraqi control on 3 September coincided with a dramatic reduction in the number of attacks on UK and Coalition Forces. From a 2007 peak of almost 120 attacks per week in late July, the number of attacks on UK and Coalition forces fell to an average of below 10 attacks per week in the six weeks after the handover of Basra Palace.[52] The MoD estimates that the handover of Basra Palace to Iraqi control was "a significant factor in this reduction" though the MoD's figures suggest that the reduction in the number of attacks against UK and Coalition Forces began in mid-August 2007, prior to the handover.[53] This would appear to reflect what we heard from local politicians in Basra, that is that much of the violence in the city was aimed at the Coalition Forces.

Table 3: Attacks on Multi-National Forces in MND(SE), January–October 2007

Source: Ministry of Defence[54]

38. In evidence to us on 23 October 2007, the Secretary of State for Defence described the security situation in Basra as "stable". Since July, he stated, the number of attacks had "gone from 401 to 19 in September".[55] Despite predictions to the contrary, he told us that the violence of the early Summer had not continued following the handover of Basra Palace and that UK Forces based at the COB at Basra Air Station were not coming under heavy or sustained attack from insurgents and militias. Similarly, Lieutenant General Peter

---

51   Q 83

52   HC (2006–07) 1091-i, Ev 19

53   *Ibid.*

54   *Ibid.*

55   *Ibid.*, Q 4

Wall, Deputy Chief of the Defence Staff (Commitments), told us that there had been a "very significant, a ten-fold reduction of activity against MNF".[56]

39. Yet despite the reduction in attacks on UK and Coalition Forces in South Eastern Iraq, the security situation in Basra remains challenging. There has been no corresponding reduction in the number of attacks aimed at civilians. The MoD's statistics reveal that the number of attacks on civilians in Basra city have "remained broadly the same". But in written evidence to us, the MoD maintained that "this is in line with our assessment that [the attacks] would stabilise [...] we still believe that over time they will reduce as the Iraqis, and the Iraqi Security Forces, grow in capability and confidence".[57] According to the MoD, the fact that there have been no increases in attacks on civilians in Basra demonstrated that "the ISF are doing an effective job of maintaining control of the city without UK support".[58]

Table 4: Attacks in MND(SE) by target, January–October 2007

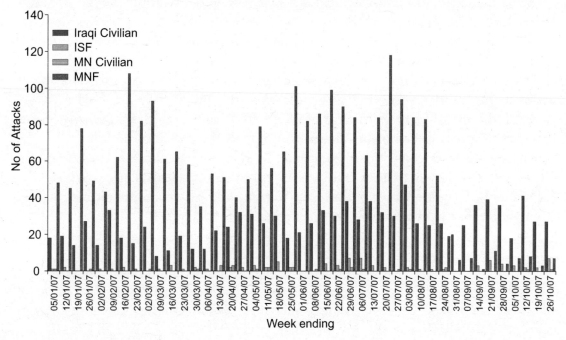

Source: Ministry of Defence[59]

40. **In the long-term stability and security in South Eastern Iraq will only come about through progress with political reconciliation. But, as at the national level, political reconciliation at the local level demands a degree of security for the political process to function.** When we visited Basra, we met a group of local politicians and discussed the security situation and the prospects of political progress in the province. We heard that Iraqi politicians had no experience of acting within a political process and that the Provincial Council lacked the authority to deal with many of the problems Iraqis faced, particularly security. We were also told that the lack of security impeded political progress.

---

56   HC (2006–07) 1091-i, Q 5

57   *Ibid.*, Ev 20

58   *Ibid.*

59   *Ibid.*

In evidence to us, the Secretary of State told us that there needed to be "more political leadership at the centre" in Baghdad and that local Shia militia groups such as Jaish Al Mahdi (JAM) needed to be brought into the political process.[60] He also stated that this could bring "the sort of sustainable progress we need" but that the UK would have "to leave the Iraqis […] the opportunity and space to do it". To this end, transition to Provincial Iraq Control would be important from a political as well as a security perspective.[61] Mr Browne also expressed optimism that in the next provincial elections, the date of which remained unclear, would deliver more representative Provincial Councils. The UK, he said, supported "early provincial elections" because:

> we believe that there would be more involvement […] if all the political parties engage in the process, then the electoral system will ensure that the provincial council is representative of the balance of political power in the area which it presently is not because people boycotted the elections in the past.[62]

41. **The reduction in the number of attacks on UK and Coalition Forces in South Eastern Iraq since August 2007 is significant. However, the fact there has been no corresponding reduction in the number of attacks against the civilian population of the city is a matter of concern. Violence in Basra Province continues to undermine the development of civil society. The relative security of Basra is said to owe more to the dominance of militias and criminal gangs, who are said to have achieved a fragile balance in the city, than to the success of the Multi-National and Iraqi Security Forces in tackling the root causes of the violence. Although the reduction in attacks on UK Forces can only be welcome, this alone cannot be a measure of success. The initial goal of UK Forces in South Eastern Iraq was to establish the security necessary for the development of representative political institutions and for economic reconstruction. Although progress has been made, this goal remains unfulfilled.**

Regional influences

42. A further factor affecting the security situation in Iraq is the nature and extent of Iranian influence. In evidence to us on 24 July 2007, the Minister for the Armed Forces made clear the destabilising effect and the extent of Iranian influence in South Eastern Iraq. He told us:

> there is clear evidence of malign influence across the border in the Basra area. There is little doubt, when you look at some of the munitions that are being used against our people, to kill our people, they are not being made in garages in down-town Basra; they are coming from outside the area.[63]

43. In his report to the US Congress in September 2007, General Petraeus presented a similar picture of malign Iranian involvement in Iraq. He argued that Iranian elements, particularly the Islamic Revolutionary Guard Corps (IRGC), had provided "training,

---

60   HC (2006–07) 1091-i, Q 45

61   *Ibid.*

62   *Ibid.*, Qq 46, 47

63   Q 164

arming, funding, and in some cases, direction of militia extremists". They had been involved in assassinating and kidnapping Iraqi government leaders. Iraqi Shia gangs had "killed and wounded our soldiers with advanced explosive devices provided by Iran". [64]General Petraeus concluded that:

> it is increasingly apparent to both Coalition and Iraqi leaders that Iran, through the use of the Qods Force, seeks to turn the Iraqi Special Groups into a Hezbollah-like force to serve its interests and fight a proxy war against the Iraqi state and coalition forces in Iraq.[65]

44. The US Ambassador to Iraq, Ryan Crocker, reported to the US Congress that "Iran plays a harmful role in Iraq". He stated:

> While claiming to support Iraq in its transition, Iran has actively undermined it by providing lethal capabilities to the enemies of the Iraqi state. In doing so, the Iranian government seems to ignore the risks that an unstable Iraq carries for its own interests.[66]

45. Academic witnesses to our inquiry offered a somewhat different analysis. Dr Herring, for example, told us that, on the basis of publicly available information, it was "inconclusive at best" that Iran was exporting Improvised Explosive Devices (IEDs) to Iraq. Indeed, Dr Herring argued that the bigger problem in Iraq was weaponry supplied by the United States to the Iraqi Police which had found its way into the hands of the militias.[67]

46. Dr Ali Ansari, of St Andrews University, told us that it was too simplistic to state that Iran was backing the insurgency in Iraq. He argued that Iran was "a very plural society" and that Western policy towards Iran had been "too monolithic". He acknowledged that the IRGC, which tended to "operate on its own agenda", was one of "the more unhelpful elements of Iranian intervention in Iraq". Some elements in Iran, he argued, sought to foster violence in Iraq so as "to make life as uncomfortable as possible" for the United States and its Coalition partners. But he also stated that there were some in the Iranian Foreign Ministry who favoured "some sort of constructive engagement with the Coalition, tacitly, behind the scenes […] to ensure that some form of stable Iraq is left, because the last thing they want is […] another Afghanistan on their Western border".[68]

47. Iranian influence in Iraq is longstanding and religious and cultural links between Iranians and Iraqis is strong, particularly in the Shia South. However, reports that elements within Iran are fuelling the violence in Iraq through the supply of arms are deeply troubling.

---

64 Report to Congress on the Situation in Iraq by General Petraeus, 10 September 2007, p 4

65 *Ibid.*

66 Report to Congress on the Situation in Iraq by Ambassador Crocker, 10 September 2007, p 4

67 Q 41

68 Q 28

3 The capacity of the Iraqi Security Forces

UK objectives in building the capacity of the ISF

48. The Prime Minister and the Secretary of State for Defence have made it clear that the change in role of UK Forces from combat operations to overwatch is dependent upon the capacity of the Iraqi Security Forces (ISF) to assume primary responsibility for security in South Eastern Iraq. The Prime Minister told the House of Commons on 8 October 2007 that "the main work of our troops is [...] to train the Iraqi Forces so that they can do the job themselves".[69] Similarly, in evidence to us on 23 October 2007, Des Browne stated that "our job is to set the conditions whereby the Iraqis can take charge of their own destiny". He emphasised that although "significant challenges" remained "there are no international or coalition resolutions to those issues; they have to be resolved by the Iraqis themselves". Mr Browne told us that "what it means in the short term is building up the Iraqi Security Forces so that increasingly they are able to take over responsibility for the security of the people without our support".[70] In written evidence to our inquiry, the Ministry of Defence stated that building and strengthening the Iraqi Security Forces was all part of the broader "coalition strategy in Iraq [...] to help to develop a functioning state".[71] Only when the Iraqi Security Forces become capable of conducting operations independently of the Multi-National Forces would UK Forces be able to complete the projected drawdown and withdraw from Iraq.

49. In our last report on Iraq, published in August 2006 following our visit to Basra and Baghdad in June 2006, we noted that UK Forces had achieved considerable successes in the training of the Iraqi Army and we expressed our hope that the 10th Division of the Iraqi Army would soon achieve full operational readiness. But we voiced our serious concerns at the level of corruption, militia infiltration and politicisation of the Iraqi Police Service. We noted that sustainable progress in increasing the capacity of the Iraqi Security Forces as a whole would only come about if problems in the Iraqi Defence and Interior Ministries were addressed.[72]

Developments at the national level

50. Recent reports have suggested that the development of the ISF has been uneven across the country and progress in building an operational capability independent of Coalition Forces inconsistent.

51. On 12 July 2007, in its Initial Benchmark Assessment Report to the US Congress, the White House concluded that "the Government of Iraq has made unsatisfactory progress toward increasing the number of ISF units capable of operating independently". Although it considered that "ISF performance has generally been adequate, particularly when units are partnered with Coalition Forces" and that the shortcomings observed did "not

---

69 HC Deb, 8 October 2007, col 27

70 HC (2006–07) 1091-i, Q 2

71 Ev 40

72 HC (2005–06) 1241, para 27

necessitate a revision to the current plan and strategy" of building the capacity of the Iraqi Security Forces, the Report concluded that "the presence of Coalition partners and support remains necessary for ISF operations".[73]

52. In August 2007, the US National Intelligence Estimate presented a similarly mixed picture of the development of the ISF. It reported that:

> Iraqi Security Forces involved in combined operations with Coalition forces have performed adequately, and some units have demonstrated increasing professional competence. However, […] the ISF have not improved enough to conduct major operations independent of the Coalition on a sustained basis in multiple locations and that the ISF remain reliant on the Coalition for important aspects of logistics and combat support.[74]

The Estimate went on to note that:

> Militia and insurgent influences continue to undermine the reliability of some ISF units, and political interference in security operations continues to undermine Coalition and ISF efforts.[75]

It concluded that, although the Maliki Government was implementing plans to expand the Iraqi Army to address "critical gaps", "significant security gains will take at least six to 12 months, and probably longer, to materialise".[76]

53. In his testimony to the US Congress on 10 September 2007, General Petraeus gave an upbeat assessment of the development of the ISF. He stated that "Iraqi Security Forces have […] continued to grow and shoulder more of the load, albeit slowly and amid continuing concerns about the sectarian tendencies of some elements in their ranks". He continued:

> Iraqi elements have been standing and fighting and sustaining tough losses, and they have taken the lead in operations in many areas […] despite their shortages, many Iraqi units now operate across Iraq with minimal coalition assistance […]Iraqi elements are slowly taking on more of the responsibility for protecting their citizens. Innumerable challenges lie ahead; however, Coalition and Iraqi Security Forces have made progress to achieving sustainable security.[77]

Iraqi Security Forces in South Eastern Iraq

The Iraqi Army

54. The MoD has presented a generally positive assessment of the development of the Iraqi Army in MND(SE). In evidence to us on 23 October 2007, Lieutenant General Wall described the UK's training and mentoring of the Iraqi Army as "a very good story".

---

73   *Initial Benchmark Assessment Report,* published by the White House, 12 July 2007, p 22

74   US National Intelligence Estimate, August 2007, p 2

75   *Ibid.,* p 3

76   US National Intelligence Estimate, August 2007, p 3

77   Report to Congress on the Situation in Iraq by General Petraeus, pp 1, 5, 6

According to Lieutenant General Wall, there had been "considerable progress" over the past year in building the capacity of the Iraqi 10th Division, the result of "quite a protracted effort" by UK and Coalition Forces, "through considerable materiel investment by, of course, the United States and some by ourselves".[78] Similarly, the Secretary of State told us that "we are making good progress across Iraq in building the capability and capacity of the security forces". The 10th Division, he argued, continued to show "its growing capability". It was now "taking the lead in many operations in the south with minimum support from the coalition"[79]:

> Overall, in the south of Iraq the Iraqi Security Forces have shown themselves as capable of dealing with isolated incidents of violence in the three provinces that have been handed over to Iraqi control and that is what they have had to face. In Basra city, they have assumed the primary role for security and they have proved able to deal efficiently with incidents of violence.[80]

55. According to Brigadier Chris Hughes, in evidence to us on 24 July 2007, the 10th Division had "had some genuine success". Overall, UK Forces had been "pleased" with its progress.[81] But he acknowledged that the Division still faced a number of challenges. Loyalty had been a particular problem but this was now being addressed through the creation of a new Division, the 14th Division, which had grown out of the 5th Brigade of the 10th Division, to operate in Basra. When we were in Iraq in July 2007 we were told that because the 10th Division was raised in Basra, the soldiers and their families were subject to intimidation and violence, and were, therefore, susceptible to intimidation and sometimes corruption. As the new 14th Division was raised in other provinces within South Eastern Iraq, the difficulties with loyalty and reliability were less likely to occur.

56. A further problem the 10th Division had encountered had been the lack of "rear end" capability, such as logistics support and intelligence assets. Although "in terms of equipment levels they are well-equipped at the moment with their frontline kit", and "have got 100% of the up-armoured Humvees that they were due to get and their other vehicles and equipment" they nevertheless lacked this important supporting capacity.[82] However, when we were in Iraq in July 2007, the UK Military Transition Team told us that the Iraqis themselves wanted additional heavy equipment. While it was recognised that Humvees were suitable for their needs they nevertheless wanted to have tanks and artillery. We also heard that it had often proved hard to unlock resources from the Iraqi Ministry of Defence. The 14th Division, in particular, was under-equipped to such an extent that militia groups and tribes had more powerful weaponry.

57. Brigadier Hughes told us that the UK Government had put £54 million through Operation OSIRIS, a project for provision of equipment and infrastructure for the Iraqi Security Forces in MND(SE). Around £13 million of this had been used to support the Iraqi Army 10th Division which was in addition to the equipment that had "flowed down

---

78   HC (2006–07) 1091-i, Q 38

79   *Ibid.*

80   *Ibid.*

81   Q 131

82   *Ibid.*

from Baghdad, originally from the Coalition and now from the Iraqi Ministry of Defence".[83] But, overall, Brigadier Hughes suggested that the 10th Division had enjoyed significant progress:

> Are they a reasonable force, given where they have come from in the timeframe that they have come from, yes they are. Do they have problems? Yes, they do [...] They continue to be taken forward and [...] we continue with the SSR [Security Sector Reform] process.[84]

58. One significant development over the past year was the appointment of General Mohan as Commander of Iraqi Security Forces in Basra Province. According to the Secretary of State, General Mohan had "brought strong Iraqi leadership to the security situation in Basra" which was "extremely welcome from our perspective" as he "takes a very robust approach to the development of the Iraqi Security Forces as a whole".[85] The Minister for the Armed Forces told us in July 2007 that he believed that the appointment of General Mohan was "very important" and "a good sign of potential" for improving the leadership of the Iraqi Army.[86] According to Mr Ainsworth, the appointment, together with that of General Jalil to command the Iraqi Police in South Eastern Iraq, amounted to a "recognition" by the Iraqis "that their getting a grip of their security arrangements in Basra is increasingly important and that we are not prepared to hold on forever". There had, he suggested, been "a concentration of the mind" among Iraqis in the South of the country.[87]

59. **There has been significant progress over the course of the past year in building the capacity of the Iraqi Army in South Eastern Iraq. Major improvements have been made to the capacity and readiness of the 10th Division, to its ability to operate independently of the Multi-National Forces, and to the equipment made available to it. We welcome the creation of the new 14th Division for Basra as a way of addressing the problem of loyalty which had confronted the largely Basrawi-recruited 10th Division. We also welcome the MoD's assurance that General Mohan has adopted a robust approach to the development of the Iraqi Security Forces in Basra. But the job is not yet complete. Despite its increasing capability, the Iraqi Army in South Eastern Iraq still requires the support of UK Forces, particularly in logistics and intelligence. The MoD should explain in its response to this report how it is addressing this lack of "rear end" capability in the Iraqi Army, when it expects this capability gap to be filled, and for how long it expects UK Forces to be required to lend support to the Iraqi Army. We also call upon the MoD to provide in its response an analysis of UK expenditure on, and the results of, projects for the provision of equipment and infrastructure to the Iraqi Security Forces, including Operation OSIRIS.**

---

83   Q 131

84   *Ibid.*

85   HC (2006–07) 1091-i, Q 38

86   Q 83

87   Q 96

The Iraqi Police Service

60. The development of the Iraqi Police Service stands in marked contrast to the development of the Iraqi Army. There continue to be serious problems of corruption and militia infiltration, and the loyalty and affiliation of many police officers remain in question. In evidence to us Dr Dodge suggested that the training of the Iraqi Police had been "an abject failure". He stated that "the Police are responsible for a great deal of kidnapping in Baghdad and have been thoroughly penetrated by the militias in the South".[88] According to Dr Dodge, the reform of the Police compared very poorly with that of the Army:

> although there are undoubtedly problems in the Army, they are much, much less, and if you look at opinion poll data [...] the Army consistently gets a much higher recognition of trust than the Police Force, which, again, not detracting from the problems inside the Army, indicates the Army has more professionalism [...] although the Army has problems, it is more coherent, a more nationalist force than the Police themselves.[89]

61. Dr Herring suggested that the emphasis on the training of the Police, like the Army, missed the point; "training", he argued, "is not the issue, loyalty is the issue". The Iraqi Security Forces as a whole were "riddled with [...] embedded insurgents" and "we are not going to train that out of them".[90]

62. The Ministry of Defence accepts that the development of the Iraqi Police has not been as successful as the development of the Iraqi Army. In evidence to us on 23 October 2007, the Secretary of State acknowledged that there was "no question" that there was "an endemic level of corruption in the police".[91] Similarly, the Minister for the Armed Forces told us in July that "progress with regards to army capability and army capacity is a lot more reassuring than it is in the area of the police". He stated that "the police have got a lot more work to do" and that "the problems are far deeper and more difficult to deal with".[92] According to Brigadier Hughes, the Iraqi Police Service was the "biggest challenge". There was "effectively [...] a small, murderous, criminal element within the Iraqi Police Force which we have to root out [...] because they are truly irreconcilable".[93]

63. The MoD maintains that the appointment of General Jalil to command the police in Basra Province is a positive step and one that is beginning to deliver results, albeit slowly. In a memorandum to us, the MoD stated that General Jalil "has shown much determination to reform the Iraqi Police Service in [Basra] province" and was committed to the "aim of building an independent, loyal police force". According to the MoD, General Jalil's efforts to root out corruption had already led to the dismissal of a total of 111 officers for corrupt activity, including affiliation with militias and a further 40 officers were under

---

88 Q 58

89 Q 59

90 Q 58

91 HC (2006–07) 1091-i, Q 41

92 Q 83

93 Q 131

investigation by the Province's Department of Internal Affairs. The Government of Iraq, which holds responsibility for the Police in the other three provinces of MND(SE), had dismissed over 2,000 police officers since August 2006.[94] According to the Secretary of State, there was "very strong evidence" that General Jalil was "building […] an independent and loyal force which is increasingly capable of serving the people at Basra and patrolling the streets". General Jalil and his family had become a target for attacks by those opposed to his attempt to root out corruption and militia infiltration.[95]

64. **The development of the Iraqi Army and the Iraqi Police Service as credible, capable, and effective Forces, which enjoy the confidence and support of the Iraqi people, is fundamental to the long-term security of Iraq and to the drawdown and eventual withdrawal of UK Forces. If Iraq is to evolve into a stable, functioning and prosperous country, the Iraqi Army and Police must be properly equipped and trained. The Iraqi Government must ensure that corruption and militia infiltration are rooted out and that the Army and Police are properly supported by the Defence and Interior Ministries. We call upon the MoD to explain in its response to this report how the training of the Iraqi Security Forces—both the Army and the Police—will progress once the number of UK Forces in Iraq has been reduced to 2,500.**

65. **While we welcome the efforts reported to have been made by General Jalil to counter murderous, corrupt, and militia-infiltrated elements within the police in Basra, we remain concerned about the present state of the Iraqi Police. Progress with reforms has been painfully slow and serious questions appear to remain about the loyalty of a significant number of officers. Unlike the Army, which shows clear signs of progress in achieving operational independence, the Police would seem to have a long way to go in becoming truly effective and in gaining the trust of the population. Given the scale of the problems which still need to be tackled, there would seem to be a need for an ongoing commitment by the UK to training and mentoring the Iraqi Police. We call upon the MoD to explain in its response to this report how it proposes to continue its mentoring and training programme following the proposed reduction of UK Forces.**

94   HC (2006–07) 1091-i, Ev 21

95   *Ibid.*, Q 41

4 The role of UK Forces in Iraq

Equipment issues

66. In our last report on UK operations in Iraq, published on 10 August 2006, we expressed our concerns about the equipment shortages and deficiencies facing UK Forces in Iraq. We were concerned about the vulnerability of UK Forces travelling in Snatch Land Rovers and called upon the MoD to review the use of these vehicles and consider "off the shelf" purchases to address the problem. We also expressed our concern at the shortage of helicopters in theatre and the pressures on air and ground crew which resulted from these shortages. We called upon the MoD to examine the problem of helicopter availability as a matter of priority. We highlighted the poor reliability of the airbridge carrying troops into theatre and stated that it was unacceptable that Servicemen and women, many of whom were serving greatly in excess of their Harmony Guidelines, should have their leave disrupted by the MoD's inability to provide a reliable airbridge. We also noted that UK Forces in Iraq had expressed their concerns about the structure and level of their allowances and had reported to us that there was insufficient financial recognition of their service while on operations. Finally, we observed that persistent breaches of Harmony Guidelines suggested that UK Forces were overstretched.[96]

67. Over the past year, the MoD has procured 100 Mastiff armoured vehicles for deployment to Iraq and Afghanistan as well as an additional 38 Vector patrol vehicles. It has also up-armoured around 70 FV430 MK3 Bulldog tracked vehicles. In his statement to the House of Commons on 8 October 2007 the Prime Minister announced the purchase of a further 140 Mastiffs for use in both Iraq and Afghanistan.[97]

68. We asked the Minister for the Armed Forces on 24 July 2007 how the Mastiffs already deployed were performing in theatre. Mr Ainsworth told us that UK Forces had "a high degree of confidence in them" since they offered "a level of security […] that is fitting to the job they are asked to do". In evidence to us on 23 October 2007 the Secretary of State for Defence maintained that the Mastiff had proved "an astonishing success". Lieutenant General Wall said they had been "hugely successful". They had been procured and delivered quickly and had been readily integrated into the day-to-day business of UK Forces in Iraq.

69. In written evidence to us, the MoD argued that the Urgent Operational Requirement (UOR) process was working well in "rapidly delivering to the front line the battle-winning capability required by our Armed Forces". It stated that as of August 2007, "91% of all equipment procured under the UOR process was deemed either highly effective or effective by troops in theatre".[98] The Secretary of State told us that UK Forces in theatre were now better equipped than ever before. The MoD was "learning lessons" about the impact of using its equipment in harsh environments which "take their toll on the vehicles" and "on

---

96   HC (2005–06) 1241, paras 51–82

97   HC Deb, 8 October 2007, col 24

98   HC (2006–07) 1091-i, Ev 37

those who maintain them". Mr Browne said that these lessons were being fed into the MoD's long-term procurement programmes.[99]

70. The Secretary of State also told us that the availability of helicopters was improving. He announced in March 2007 that the UK would convert eight Chinooks and purchase six additional Merlin helicopters which would "increase our Chinook and Merlin fleets capability by 20% and 25% respectively.[100] The Minister for the Armed Forces told the House on 9 October 2007 that "we expect all six Merlins to be operational next year".[101] In a written statement, Mr Ainsworth told the House that "on current plans we expect to see the [Chinook] aircraft delivered by the end of 2009".[102] **It will be important for the MoD to monitor closely the progress of the Merlin and Chinook programmes and, if necessary, take appropriate action to prevent slippage so that these helicopters are available for operational use as soon as possible.**

71. We examined the issue of the airbridge in our Strategic Lift report published on 5 July 2007. In the report we highlighted the good performance of the C-17 large transport aircraft and recommended that "given the performance of its C-17 large transport aircraft, the MoD must give consideration to the acquisition of additional C-17 aircraft".[103] The Government Response to our report stated that:

> The Department agrees the recommendation. The C-17 has proved a great success on operations and we keep our C-17 requirements under continual review.... On 26 July 2007 the MoD announced its intention to purchase a sixth Boeing C-17 Globemaster III, as part of a number of measures to enhance operational effectiveness.[104]

72. **We welcome the deployment of additional armoured vehicles to our Forces in Iraq and are reassured that the Urgent Operational Requirement (UOR) process is delivering much needed equipment to our Forces in theatre. The deployment of additional Mastiff and Bulldog armoured vehicles has significantly improved the force protection available to our Forces in Iraq. However, we are concerned that current operations are reducing the planned lives of equipment and that this could lead to potential capability gaps in the future. We are also concerned that equipment returning from operational theatres—whether it was procured through the routine acquisition process or as UORs—will require substantial expenditure to repair, refurbish, support and store, and it appears that no provision has been made for this in the MoD's budget. This will make the management of the MoD's budget increasingly difficult. We expect the MoD, in its response to our report, to set out how it plans to address any capability gaps arising from the intensive use of equipment on current operations, its estimate of**

---

99   HC (2006–07) 1091-i, Q 91

100 *Ibid.*, Q 92

101 HC Deb, 9 October 2007, col 200

102 HC Deb, 8 October 2007, col 73 WS

103 Defence Committee, Eleventh Report of Session 2006–07, *Strategic Lift,* HC 462, para 67

104 Defence Committee, Fourteenth Special Report of Session 2006–07, *Strategic Lift: Government Response to the Committee's Eleventh Report of Session 2006–07,* HC 1025, para 12

the costs needed for repairing and refurbishing equipment returning from operational theatres, and how this will be funded.

73. **We also welcome the planned increase in the number of Chinook and Merlin helicopters. This should improve helicopter availability when these helicopters become available for operational use over the next two years. The purchase of an additional C-17 large transport aircraft will further improve the MoD's strategic air-lift capability and we look forward to receiving the MoD's end-to-end review of the airbridge—the Air Movements Process Study—when it is published in December 2007. We will continue to monitor the MoD's equipment programme, the support to troops in theatre, and the impact of the current high tempo of operation on our Forces in our current inquiries into Defence Equipment and the MoD's Annual Report and Accounts.**

Internment and detention

74. In our report last year we noted that UK Forces in Iraq maintained a Divisional Temporary Detention Facility (DTDF) at the Shaibah Logistics Base, housing people considered to be a threat to security, under the authority of United Nations Security Council Resolution 1637. We called upon the MoD to make public, on a regular basis, the number of detainees held by UK Forces in Iraq, and the grounds for detention. We emphasised that detention without trial was, of itself, undesirable, though we understood the reasons for it.[105]

75. The MoD's written evidence of 10 September 2007 distinguished between detention (defined as the period during which a person is held by MNF following arrest, until he is either transferred to the Iraqi judicial system, or released, or a decision is made by MNF to hold him as an internee) and internment (defined as the longer-term holding of an individual by MNF where it is judged that this is necessary for imperative reasons of security). The MoD stated:

> Any individual detained by UK forces will have his case reviewed by the Divisional Internment Review Committee (DIRC) […] within 48 hours of initial detention and a decision as to whether internment is necessary will be taken. Individuals are only interned where the DIRC judges that they pose an imperative threat to security.[106]

76. Following the handover to Iraqi control of Shaibah Logistics Base, UK internees are now held in the purpose-built Divisional Internment Facility (DIF) at Basra Air Station. The MoD's written evidence stated that, at the end of July 2007, the UK held 86 individuals at the DIF, of which: 1 had been convicted by the Central Criminal Court of Iraq (CCCI) and was awaiting transfer to the Iraqi Authorities; 10 were awaiting trial in the CCCI; and 75 were security internees. In contrast, at mid-August 2007, the US held around 20,000 internees in their in-theatre internment facilities in Iraq.[107]

---

105 HC (2005–06) 1241, paras 39–46

106 Ev 36

107 *Ibid.*

77. The MoD argued that internment without trial continues to be necessary because:

> there are still individuals in Iraq whose aim is to undermine the establishment of democratic rule through violence directed at MNF, the Iraqi Security Forces and Iraqi civilians. Internment is used sparingly and only when individuals present an imperative threat to security. Additionally, we need to continue to hold those who have perpetrated attacks against us in the past and who we believe remain a threat to security. Further, internment is in the interest of the Iraqi civilian population and is for their protection as well as our own.[108]

78. The written evidence from the Redress Trust raised a number of concerns about detention and internment by UK forces in Iraq. Drawing on the evidence presented to the court martial *R v Payne & Others*, relating to the death of Baha Musa and the alleged mistreatment of other Iraqi civilians in Basra during September 2003, it expressed concern about the holding and questioning of detainees at the battlegroup level, in the period between capture and delivery to the central detention facility. It questioned whether the MoD's doctrine on prisoner of war and civilian detainee and internee handling had been fully implemented, and whether interrogators were given up-to-date training, And it asked for clarification about the role of medical staff before, during and after questioning.[109] **The detention of Iraqis without trial is a matter of public concern. We call on the MoD to respond in its response to this report to the questions raised by the Redress Trust about the handling of detainees in Iraq.**

The changing footprint of UK Forces in South Eastern Iraq

79. The reductions in the number of UK military personnel serving in Iraq during the course of 2007 reflects the changing footprint of UK Forces. Until early 2007, UK and Coalition Forces were stationed at several bases in and around Basra City: the Old State Building, the Shatt-Al-Arab Hotel, Shaibah Logistics Base, the Provincial Joint Co-ordination Centre at Basra Palace and the Contingency Operating Base at Basra Air Station.

80. With the exception of Basra Air Station, all UK and Coalition bases in South Eastern Iraq have now been handed over to local Iraqi control. On 20 February 2007, command of the 10th Division of the Iraqi Army was handed over to local Iraqi control. On 20 March 2007, UK Forces handed over control of the Old State Building to the Iraqi Army 10th Division, the first Coalition base to be transferred.[110] On 8 April, the Shatt-Al-Arab Hotel, which had been the main base from which operations in the northern part of Basra City had been mounted, was handed to Iraqi control and later that month, on 24 April, Shaibah Logistics Base, a major UK base on the outskirts of Basra City, was handed over to the Iraqis. Most recently, on 3 September, UK Forces completed the handover of Basra Palace, the last Coalition base inside Basra City. UK and Coalition Forces in South Eastern Iraq are now all based at the Contingency Operating Base Basra Air Station.

---

108 Ev 37

109 Ev 41–43

110 UK and Coalition Forces handed over control of Camp Smitty in Al Muthanna and Camp Abu Naji in Maysan to Iraqi control on 30 July and 30 August 2006 respectively.

81. The consolidation of UK and Coalition Forces at the COB at Basra Air Station followed the transition of three of the four provinces in the UK's area of operations to Provincial Iraqi Control. Al Muthanna and Dhi Qar provinces were transferred to Iraqi control in July and September 2006 respectively. Maysan Province was transferred to Iraqi control in April 2007. On 30 October 2007, the Iraqi Prime Minister, Nouri Al-Maliki announced that the Iraqi Army would assume control of Basra Province from UK Forces in December 2007.[111]

Table 5: Key dates in transition to Iraqi control in MND(SE)

Date of handover to Iraqi control	Province / Base / Division
13 July 2006	Al Muthanna Province
30 July 2006	Camp Smitty, Al Muthanna
30 August 2006	Camp Abu Naji, Maysan
21 September 2006	Dhi Qar Province
20 December 2006	An-Najaf Province (in MND (Centre South))
20 February 2007	Command of Iraqi Army 10th Division
20 March 2007	Old State Building, Basra City
8 April 2007	Shatt-Al-Arab Hotel, Basra City
18 April 2007	Maysan Province
24 April 2007	Shaibah Logistics Base
3 September 2007	Basra Palace
December 2007*	Basra Province

* Projected date.

Source: Ministry of Defence[112]

The changing role of UK Forces

82. The impending handover of Basra Province to Iraqi control, scheduled for December 2007, will presage a change in the role of UK Forces in South Eastern Iraq. In a statement to the House of Commons on 8 October 2007, the Prime Minister announced that "the next important stage in delivering our strategy to hand over security to the Iraqis is to move from a combat role in the rest of Basra province to overwatch" across the whole of South Eastern Iraq and transferring overall responsibility for security to Iraqi control. Switching to a position of overwatch, the Prime Minister stated, would have two stages:

> In the first, British forces that remain in Iraq will have the following tasks: training and mentoring the Iraqi army and police force; securing supply routes and policing

111 Ministry of Defence press notice, 30 October 2007

112 Ministry of Defence website (www.mod.uk)

the Iran-Iraq border; and the ability to come to the assistance of the Iraqi security forces when called upon. Then in the Spring of next year—and guided as always by the advice of our military commanders—we plan to move to a second stage of overwatch where the coalition would maintain a more limited re-intervention capacity and where the main focus would be on training and mentoring.[113]

83. The Prime Minister outlined the implications of the transition to overwatch for the number of UK Forces deployed in Iraq:

> We plan from next Spring to reduce our force numbers in southern Iraq to a figure of 2,500. The first stage begins now. With the Iraqis already assuming security responsibility, we expect to: establish provincial Iraqi control in Basra province in the next two months [...] move to the first stage of overwatch; reduce numbers in southern Iraq from 5,500 at the start of September to 4,500 immediately after provincial Iraqi control and then to 4,000; and then in the second stage of overwatch from the Spring [...] reduce to around 2,500 troops, with a further decision about the next phase made then. In both stages of overwatch, around 500 logistics and support personnel will be based outside Iraq but elsewhere in the region.[114]

Table 6: Projected reductions in UK force levels from September 2007

Date	Number of troops
September 2007	5,500
November 2007	5,000
Christmas 2007	4,500
From Spring 2008	2,500

Source: Ministry of Defence[115]

84. In a joint statement on 31 October 2007, welcoming the Iraqi Prime Minister's announcement that Basra Province would be transferred to Iraqi control in December 2007, the Defence Secretary, Des Browne, and the Foreign Secretary, Rt Hon David Miliband MP, emphasised that "the transition of Basra does not signal the end of our commitment to the people of Iraq". Instead, "it now enters a new stage" in which:

> we will continue to train and mentor the Iraqi Security Forces and we will protect the border and supply routes, while retaining the capability to support the Iraqis directly if so requested. But the Iraqis will take the lead, as they have proved more than capable of doing in Muthanna, Dhi Qar and Maysan.[116]

Despite ceding control for security in the region to the Iraqis, Mr Browne and Mr Miliband emphasised that the UK would "remain closely engaged with the Government of Iraq to

---

113 HC Deb, 8 October 2007, col 23

114 *Ibid.*

115 HC Deb, 8 October 2007, col 21

116 Ministry of Defence press release, 31 October 2007

promote national reconciliation, and to ensure the development of a diverse and strong economy".[117]

85. Until now, UK Forces in South Eastern Iraq have held overall responsibility for security in Basra. As the Minister for the Armed Forces told us in evidence on 24 July, "we are [...] the ultimate guarantor of any chance of progress" in South Eastern Iraq.[118] With the switch to overwatch, this would change. Iraqis themselves would assume responsibility for security across the whole of MND(SE).

86. Mr Ainsworth defined overwatch as "being there, able in the absolute extreme to offer support, but to stand back and allow the Iraqi forces themselves to try and deal with the situations that arise".[119] In written evidence to our inquiry, the MoD explained that overwatch is "a term specific to UK forces" within MND(SE) which "is used to describe the force structure for a given province" and "is subdivided into 3 phases: tactical, operational and strategic".[120] At the tactical stage of overwatch, UK Forces remain responsible for security:

> Initially, they are responsible for the routine provision of security. Over time, routine and non-essential Multi-National Force (MNF) activity progressively reduces, as Iraqi Security Forces (ISF) take increasing responsibility for providing security as a means of moving towards security self-reliance.[121]

87. The operational phase of overwatch takes place after the transfer to Provincial Iraqi Control. According to the MoD, in this posture UK and Coalition Forces "provide a re-intervention capability, but the requirement to intervene will be only *in extremis* and at the request of the Iraqi authorities". The principal focus of UK Forces during this period is on security sector reform: the training and mentoring of the Iraqi Security Forces, particularly the Iraqi Army. Nevertheless, the UK continues to protect "key supply routes" and "points of entry". This is the current stage of overwatch in Al Muthanna, Dhi Qar and Maysan provinces, and will also be the case in Basra Province following transition to Provincial Iraqi Control which is scheduled for December 2007.[122]

88. The MoD describes the final stage of overwatch as "strategic overwatch". During this period, the UK and Coalition effort "will move to supporting the Iraqi Government and Security Forces in facing strategic threats to their internal and external security".[123]

89. The MoD envisages regional variations across South Eastern Iraq. In evidence to us on 24 July, Brigadier Hughes told us that:

> What we do not envisage in overwatch is one package fits all, so if the Iraqi Security Forces were going to ask us for support once they have got provincial control, we do

---

117 Ministry of Defence press release, 31 October 2007

118 Q 83

119 Q 121

120 Ev 39

121 *Ibid.*

122 Ev 40

123 *Ibid.*

not envisage them necessarily meaning that we have got to put a battle group into the middle of the city. What they might be short of is intelligence and surveillance assets, so it might be just flying something high up, or it might be another niche capability or a piece of logistics that they need putting in place. We foresee in over-watch maybe nothing or maybe very limited and a scaled approach to it.[124]

90. **As the UK moves towards full operational overwatch in South Eastern Iraq, the key issues are how many troops will be needed in theatre, whether overwatch could be performed outside Iraq, and whether the UK might need to maintain a reserve of troops to re-intervene if the security situation in South Eastern Iraq deteriorated significantly.**

91. In July 2007 the Minister for the Armed Forces told us that, in order to perform effective overwatch, a force of around 5,000 would be required. Anything below this number would prove difficult to sustain:

> The force is not self-sustaining and able to protect itself and do all the other work it has to do below about 5,000, so we are approaching levels where we cannot go much further […] in an actual overwatch situation we cannot go much below 5,000 because we have to sustain the force and self-protect the force itself, so overwatch itself does not take us down a lot further than that.[125]

92. Mr Ainsworth's suggestion that a force package of around 5,000 represented a minimum sustainable number reflects what we heard during our visit to Iraq in July 2007. During our visit, we were told that minimum force levels had already been reached. Although limited reductions might prove possible following the transition of Basra Palace to Iraq control, there remained a critical mass of around 4,000 to 5,000 below which the sustainability of the force package would be called into question. We heard that any further reductions would mean that the remaining UK Force would be able to do little more than sustain and protect itself at the Contingency Operating Base at Basra Air Station.

93. In his statement to the House of Commons on 8 October, however, the Prime Minister announced plans to reduce UK force levels in Iraq to 4,500 following the transfer of Basra Province to Iraqi control in December 2007 and, shortly thereafter, to 4,000 in the first stage of overwatch and to 2,500 in the second stage of overwatch "from the Spring of 2008".[126]

94. We asked the Secretary of State for Defence about the apparent discrepancy between the Prime Minister's announcement in October 2007 of a reduction in UK force levels to 2,500 from the Spring of 2008 and the Minister for the Armed Forces' suggestion, in July 2007, that a force package much below 5,000 would not be sustainable. Mr Browne denied that there were any discrepancy and told us that:

> what has changed is that we are now in a position to have a very clear idea, in consultation with our allies and with the Iraqis themselves, as to exactly what we will

---

124 Q 130

125 Q 120

126 HC Deb, 8 October 2007, col 23

be doing and what tasks we will be carrying out and we plan the number of troops in relation to the tasks, so the tasks have changed.[127]

Mr Browne added that he was satisfied that on the basis of the evidence he had received the Prime Minister's "figure of troops to tasks is the right figure". That figure was "a product of a close assessment of our future requirement" and "the key to this figure has been the judgment of the military commanders".[128] The MoD subsequently provided us with classified written evidence addressing the tasks that UK and Coalition Forces would be required to fulfil following the transition of security responsibility in Basra to Provincial Iraqi Control and the number of troops that will be required to fulfil those tasks.

95. Lieutenant General Wall maintained that the proposed reductions in UK Forces in Iraq were not the result of overstretch. According to Lieutenant General Wall, "this has not been driven by what is available". He maintained that "were more forces needed at this stage of the campaign […] the Army could provide additional forces […] That is not to say it will not benefit from a reduction".[129] Reducing the UK military commitment to 2,500 was "perfectly workable in light of the tasks that we envisage". The reduction would mean a that the number of Battlegroups in theatre would be cut from four to two. However, the difference in the number of Battlegroups could be "accounted for in terms of the change of tasks […] as we go increasingly towards a mentoring and supporting role rather than that which we are engaged in at the moment".[130] Nevertheless, Lieutenant General Wall maintained that, even after the drawdown of Forces, the UK would still be capable of deploying a Battlegroup in a combat role if the security situation so demanded.[131]

96. We also asked the Secretary of State whether, in light of the proposed reductions, UK Forces could be re-deployed to Iraq if the security situation were to deteriorate significantly. Lieutenant General Wall maintained that reinforcements could be found from a variety of sources, from Iraqi, Coalition, and UK Forces:

> If it is a question of delivering reserves into the MND South East area in response to requests from the Iraqi agencies and presumably at that stage through the Iraqi MoD with the Iraqi Prime Minister's endorsement, then there are a number of levels at which those reserves could be delivered, starting with the Iraqi security forces themselves, we could redeploy into the area either from elsewhere in the south or from nationwide, the MNF core-level reserves […] or indeed, if required and in extremis, additional UK forces from our own reserves.[132]

Lieutenant General Wall stated that there were sufficient UK Forces to replenish and reinforce those in Iraq if needed, irrespective of what happened in Afghanistan.

97. **The MoD has said that, despite transferring security responsibility to the Iraqi Security Forces, UK Forces will retain the capability to re-intervene in South Eastern**

---

127 HC (2006–07) 1091-i, Q 8

128 *Ibid.*, Q 9

129 *Ibid.*, Q 13

130 *Ibid.*, Q 14

131 *Ibid.*, Q 15

132 *Ibid.*, Q 21

Iraq if the security situation deteriorates. If that re-intervention capability is to be credible the UK will need to be capable of drawing upon Forces from outside Iraq. We call upon the MoD to clarify how it plans to maintain a re-intervention capacity, which Forces would be assigned to that role, and where they would be based.

98. The Prime Minister's announcement that the number of UK Forces in Iraq will be reduced to 2,500 from the Spring of 2008 is noted, but important questions remain about the sustainability of a force of this size. If there is still a role for UK Forces in Iraq, those Forces must be capable of doing more than just protecting themselves at Basra Air Station. If the reduction in numbers means they cannot do more than this, the entire UK presence in South Eastern Iraq will be open to question.

Conclusions and recommendations

1. The fact that this report does not comment on the progress of maritime operations in Iraqi waters is not a reflection of the relative importance we attach to those operations. We acknowledge the important contribution which all three Services are making to the security of the region. (Paragraph 12)

2. We note the progress of the US surge in and around Baghdad and welcome the apparent reductions in the level of violence, both against Coalition and Iraqi Forces and the civilian population. But it is important not to overstate the successes of the surge. The level of violence in Iraq is still worryingly high. It remains to be seen whether the improvements in the security situation represent a lasting reduction in insurgent, militia and sectarian violence or whether the violence will once again increase after the US withdraws the surge element of its Forces. (Paragraph 26)

3. The Iraqi Government must make the most of the reduction in violence to move the political process forward to achieve meaningful and lasting political reconciliation in Iraq. In the long-term, it is only through reconciliation, both nationally and locally, that Iraq can develop into a secure and stable country. (Paragraph 27)

4. In the long-term stability and security in South Eastern Iraq will only come about through progress with political reconciliation. But, as at the national level, political reconciliation at the local level demands a degree of security for the political process to function. (Paragraph 40)

5. The reduction in the number of attacks on UK and Coalition Forces in South Eastern Iraq since August 2007 is significant. However, the fact there has been no corresponding reduction in the number of attacks against the civilian population of the city is a matter of concern. Violence in Basra Province continues to undermine the development of civil society. The relative security of Basra is said to owe more to the dominance of militias and criminal gangs, who are said to have achieved a fragile balance in the city, than to the success of the Multi-National and Iraqi Security Forces in tackling the root causes of the violence. Although the reduction in attacks on UK Forces can only be welcome, this alone cannot be a measure of success. The initial goal of UK Forces in South Eastern Iraq was to establish the security necessary for the development of representative political institutions and for economic reconstruction. Although progress has been made, this goal remains unfulfilled. (Paragraph 41)

6. Iranian influence in Iraq is longstanding and religious and cultural links between Iranians and Iraqis is strong, particularly in the Shia South. However, reports that elements within Iran are fuelling the violence in Iraq through the supply of arms are deeply troubling. (Paragraph 47)

7. There has been significant progress over the course of the past year in building the capacity of the Iraqi Army in South Eastern Iraq. Major improvements have been made to the capacity and readiness of the 10th Division, to its ability to operate independently of the Multi-National Forces, and to the equipment made available to

it. We welcome the creation of the new 14th Division for Basra as a way of addressing the problem of loyalty which had confronted the largely Basrawi-recruited 10th Division. We also welcome the MoD's assurance that General Mohan has adopted a robust approach to the development of the Iraqi Security Forces in Basra. But the job is not yet complete. Despite its increasing capability, the Iraqi Army in South Eastern Iraq still requires the support of UK Forces, particularly in logistics and intelligence. The MoD should explain in its response to this report how it is addressing this lack of "rear end" capability in the Iraqi Army, when it expects this capability gap to be filled, and for how long it expects UK Forces to be required to lend support to the Iraqi Army. We also call upon the MoD to provide in its response an analysis of UK expenditure on, and the results of, projects for the provision of equipment and infrastructure to the Iraqi Security Forces, including Operation OSIRIS. (Paragraph 59)

8. The development of the Iraqi Army and the Iraqi Police Service as credible, capable, and effective Forces, which enjoy the confidence and support of the Iraqi people, is fundamental to the long-term security of Iraq and to the drawdown and eventual withdrawal of UK Forces. If Iraq is to evolve into a stable, functioning and prosperous country, the Iraqi Army and Police must be properly equipped and trained. The Iraqi Government must ensure that corruption and militia infiltration are rooted out and that the Army and Police are properly supported by the Defence and Interior Ministries. We call upon the MoD to explain in its response to this report how the training of the Iraqi Security Forces—both the Army and the Police—will progress once the number of UK Forces in Iraq has been reduced to 2,500. (Paragraph 64)

9. While we welcome the efforts reported to have been made by General Jalil to counter murderous, corrupt, and militia-infiltrated elements within the police in Basra, we remain concerned about the present state of the Iraqi Police. Progress with reforms has been painfully slow and serious questions appear to remain about the loyalty of a significant number of officers. Unlike the Army, which shows clear signs of progress in achieving operational independence, the Police would seem to have a long way to go in becoming truly effective and in gaining the trust of the population. Given the scale of the problems which still need to be tackled, there would seem to be a need for an ongoing commitment by the UK to training and mentoring the Iraqi Police. We call upon the MoD to explain in its response to this report how it proposes to continue its mentoring and training programme following the proposed reduction of UK Forces. (Paragraph 65)

10. It will be important for the MoD to monitor closely the progress of the Merlin and Chinook programmes and, if necessary, take appropriate action to prevent slippage so that these helicopters are available for operational use as soon as possible. (Paragraph 70)

11. We welcome the deployment of additional armoured vehicles to our Forces in Iraq and are reassured that the Urgent Operational Requirement (UOR) process is delivering much needed equipment to our Forces in theatre. The deployment of additional Mastiff and Bulldog armoured vehicles has significantly improved the force protection available to our Forces in Iraq. However, we are concerned that

current operations are reducing the planned lives of equipment and that this could lead to potential capability gaps in the future. We are also concerned that equipment returning from operational theatres—whether it was procured through the routine acquisition process or as UORs—will require substantial expenditure to repair, refurbish, support and store, and it appears that no provision has been made for this in the MoD's budget. This will make the management of the MoD's budget increasingly difficult. We expect the MoD, in its response to our report, to set out how it plans to address any capability gaps arising from the intensive use of equipment on current operations, its estimate of the costs needed for repairing and refurbishing equipment returning from operational theatres, and how this will be funded. (Paragraph 72)

12. We also welcome the planned increase in the number of Chinook and Merlin helicopters. This should improve helicopter availability when these helicopters become available for operational use over the next two years. The purchase of an additional C-17 large transport aircraft will further improve the MoD's strategic air-lift capability and we look forward to receiving the MoD's end-to-end review of the airbridge—the Air Movements Process Study—when it is published in December 2007. We will continue to monitor the MoD's equipment programme, the support to troops in theatre, and the impact of the current high tempo of operation on our Forces in our current inquiries into Defence Equipment and the MoD's Annual Report and Accounts. (Paragraph 73)

13. The detention of Iraqis without trial is a matter of public concern. We call on the MoD to respond in its response to this report to the questions raised by the Redress Trust about the handling of detainees in Iraq. (Paragraph 78)

14. As the UK moves towards full operational overwatch in South Eastern Iraq, the key issues are how many troops will be needed in theatre, whether overwatch could be performed outside Iraq, and whether the UK might need to maintain a reserve of troops to re-intervene if the security situation in South Eastern Iraq deteriorated significantly. (Paragraph 90)

15. The MoD has said that, despite transferring security responsibility to the Iraqi Security Forces, UK Forces will retain the capability to re-intervene in South Eastern Iraq if the security situation deteriorates. If that re-intervention capability is to be credible the UK will need to be capable of drawing upon Forces from outside Iraq. We call upon the MoD to clarify how it plans to maintain a re-intervention capacity, which Forces would be assigned to that role, and where they would be based. (Paragraph 97)

16. The Prime Minister's announcement that the number of UK Forces in Iraq will be reduced to 2,500 from the Spring of 2008 is noted, but important questions remain about the sustainability of a force of this size. If there is still a role for UK Forces in Iraq, those Forces must be capable of doing more than just protecting themselves at Basra Air Station. If the reduction in numbers means they cannot do more than this, the entire UK presence in South Eastern Iraq will be open to question. (Paragraph 98)

Annex A: List of Abbreviations

AOR	Area of Responsibility
AQI	Al Qaeda Iraq
CCCI	Central Criminal Court of Iraq
COB	Contingency Operating Base (Basra Air Station)
DIF	Divisional Internment Facility
DIRC	Divisional Internment Review Committee
IED	Improvised Explosive Device
IPS	Iraqi Police Service
IRGC	Islamic Revolutionary Guard Corps (Iran)
ISF	Iraqi Security Forces
ISG	Iraq Study Group (United States)
JAM	Jaish Al Mahdi
JHF–I	Joint Helicopter Force—Iraq
MoD	Ministry of Defence
MND(SE)	Multi-National Division (South-East)
MNF-I	Multi-National Force—Iraq
PIC	Provincial Iraqi Control
PJCC	Provincial Joint Co-ordination Centre (Basra Palace)
PRT	Provincial Reconstruction Team
SSR	Security Sector Reform
UOR	Urgent Operational Requirement
UNSCR	United Nations Security Council Resolution

Annex B: Visit to Iraq, July 2007

Members participating: Mr James Arbuthnot MP (Chairman), Mr Dai Havard MP, Mr Bernard Jenkin MP, Mr Kevan Jones MP, Willie Rennie MP and John Smith MP.

IRAQ

Basra

Sunday 8 July 2007

Basra Air Station

Briefing from Major General the Hon Jonathan Shaw, General Officer Commanding, Multi-National Division (South East)

Command briefing from Colonel Ian Thomas, Chief of Staff, MND(SE), and Major General Shaw

Briefing from HM Consul General, Mr Richard Jones

Briefing from Brigadier James Bashall, Commanding Officer, 1 Mechanised Brigade

Um Qasr

Briefing from Captain Tim Stockings RN, Commanding Officer, Naval Transition Team

Monday 9 July 2007

Basra Air Station

Briefing from Colonel Steve Shirley, Commander Force Support, and Lieutenant Colonel Rob Blackstone RE

Briefing from Group Captain Paul Burt RAF, Commander, 903 Expeditionary Air Wing, Wing Commander Tom Bunnington RAF and Wing Commander Mike Hand RAF

Briefing from Major Phil Oxley RA, Commanding Officer, 20 Battery, 16th Regiment, Royal Artillery

Briefing by Colonel Andy Bristow, Commanding Officer, 10th Iraqi Army Division Military Transition Team, Lieutenant Colonel Mark Wenham, Chief of Staff, and Brigadier General Malik Awaad Ibrahim, Deputy Commander, 10th Division, Iraq Army

Briefing from Major Dom Spencer, Officer Commanding D Company, 1 Royal Welsh, and Officer Commanding Divisional Internment Facility, and Captain Adrian Twining, Army Legal Service

Meeting with Baswari politicians

Counter-IED Briefing from Major Dave Bickles RE, Staff Officer 2 Counter Threat, 1 Mechanised Brigade

Manoeuvre Battle Group Briefing from Lieutenant Colonel James Swift, Commanding Officer, 2 Royal Welsh

Borders North Battle Group briefing by Major Andrew Horman, Second-in-Command, King's Royal Hussars

UK Medical Group Briefing by Lieutenant Colonel Toby Rowland RAMC, Commander Medical

Washup meeting with Major General Shaw

Baghdad

Tuesday 10 July 2007

British Embassy briefing from HM Ambassador the Hon Dominic Asquith CMG and Lieutenant General Graeme Lamb, Deputy Commanding General, Multi-National Force – Iraq

Meeting with the United States Ambassador to Iraq, Mr Ryan Crocker, and General David Petraeus, Commanding General, Multi-National Force – Iraq

Security transition briefing from Major General Mastin M Robeson USMC, Brigadier Neil Baverstock, Colonel Mark Castle, Chief of Campaign Plans, and Colonel J P Jenks, Chief of Intelligence Plans

Iraqi Security Forces briefing from Brigadier Stephen Glendhill

Meeting with Nouri Al-Maliki, Prime Minister of Iraq

Meeting with General Qadir Obeidir, Minister of Defence of Iraq

KUWAIT

Wednesday 11 July 2007

British Embassy Briefing from Mr Tim Stew, Chargé d'Affaires, Colonel Geoff Moynan, Defence Attaché, and Mr Jonathan Brown, Second Secretary (Political)

British Military Mission briefing from Brigadier Jamie Mackaness, Commander, British Military Mission, and Lieutenant Colonel Des Norton

Meeting with Sheikh Ali al Sabah, Deputy Head of the National Security Bureau

Meeting with Lieutenant General Fahad Ahmad al Amin, Chief of Staff, Kuwaiti Armed Forces

Meeting with Khalid Jarallah, Under-Secretary, Kuwaiti Ministry of Foreign Affairs

Formal Minutes

Tuesday 20 November 2007
[Afternoon Sitting]

Members present:

Mr James Arbuthnot, in the Chair

Mr David Crausby	Mr Brian Jenkins
Linda Gilroy	Mr Kevan Jones
Mr David Hamilton	Robert Key
Mr Dai Havard	Willie Rennie
Mr Bernard Jenkin	

UK land operations in Iraq 2007

Draft Report (UK land operations in Iraq 2007), proposed by the Chairman, brought up and read.

Ordered, That the draft Report be read a second time, paragraph by paragraph.

Paragraphs 1 to 98 read and agreed to.

Annexes [List of Abbreviations and Visit Note] and Summary agreed to.

Resolved, That the Report be the First Report of the Committee to the House.

Ordered, That the Chairman make the Report to the House.

Ordered, That embargoed copies of the Report be made available, in accordance with the provisions of Standing Order No. 134.

Written evidence was ordered to be reported to the House for printing with the Report, together with written evidence reported and ordered to be published on 24 July and 9 October.

[Adjourned till Wednesday 21 November at 9.00 am

Witnesses

List of written evidence

List of Reports from the Committee during the current Parliament

The reference number of the Government's response to each Report is printed in brackets after the HC printing number.

Session 2005–06

First Report	Armed Forces Bill	HC 747 (*HC 1021*)
Second Report	Future Carrier and Joint Combat Aircraft Programmes	HC 554 (*HC 926*)
Third Report	Delivering Front Line Capability to the RAF	HC 557 (*HC 1000*)
Fourth Report	Costs of peace-keeping in Iraq and Afghanistan: Spring Supplementary Estimate 2005–06	HC 980 (*HC 1136*)
Fifth Report	The UK deployment to Afghanistan	HC 558 (*HC 1211*)
Sixth Report	Ministry of Defence Annual Report and Accounts 2004–05	HC 822 (*HC 1293*)
Seventh Report	The Defence Industrial Strategy	HC 824 (*HC 1488*)
Eighth Report	The Future of the UK's Strategic Nuclear Deterrent: the Strategic Context	HC 986 (*HC 1558*)
Ninth Report	Ministry of Defence Main Estimates 2006–07	HC 1366 (*HC 1601*)
Tenth Report	The work of the Met Office	HC 823 (*HC 1602*)
Eleventh Report	Educating Service Children	HC 1054 (*HC 58*)
Twelfth Report	Strategic Export Controls: Annual Report for 2004, Quarterly Reports for 2005, Licensing Policy and Parliamentary Scrutiny	HC 873 (*Cm 6954*)
Thirteenth Report	UK Operations in Iraq	HC 1241 (*HC 1603*)
Fourteenth Report	Armed Forces Bill: proposal for a Service Complaints Commissioner	HC 1711 (*HC 180*)

Session 2006–07

First Report	Defence Procurement 2006	HC 56 (*HC 318*)
Second Report	Ministry of Defence Annual Report and Accounts 2005–06	HC 57 (*HC 376*)
Third Report	Costs of operations in Iraq and Afghanistan: Winter Supplementary Estimate 2006–07	HC 129 (*HC 317*)
Fourth Report	The Future of the UK's Strategic Nuclear Deterrent: the Manufacturing and Skills Base	HC 59 (*HC 304*)
Fifth Report	The work of the Committee in 2005 and 2006	HC 233 (*HC 344*)
Sixth Report	The Defence Industrial Strategy: update	HC 177 (*HC 481*)
Seventh Report	The Army's requirement for armoured vehicles: the FRES programme	HC 159 (*HC 511*)
Eighth Report	The work of the Defence Science and Technology Laboratory and the funding of defence research	HC 84 (*HC 512*)
Ninth Report	The Future of the UK's Strategic Nuclear Deterrent: the White Paper	HC 225-I and –II (*HC 551*)
Tenth Report	Cost of military operations: Spring Supplementary Estimate 2006–07	HC 379 (*HC 558*)
Eleventh Report	Strategic Lift	HC 462 *(HC1025)*
Twelfth Report	Ministry of Defence Main Estimates 2007–08	HC 835 *(HC 1026)*
Thirteenth Report	UK operations in Afghanistan	HC 408 *(HC 1024)*
Fourteenth Report	Strategic Export Controls: 2007 Review	HC 117 *(Cm 7260)*
Fifteenth Report	The work of Defence Estates	HC 535 *(HC 109)*

Oral evidence

Taken before the Defence Committee

on Tuesday 26 June 2007

Members present

Mr James Arbuthnot, in the Chair

Mr David S Borrow	Mr Bernard Jenkin
Mr David Crausby	Mr Brian Jenkins
Linda Gilroy	Robert Key
Mr David Hamilton	Willie Rennie
Mr Adam Holloway	John Smith

Witnesses: **Dr Ali Ansari**, University of St Andrews, **Dr Toby Dodge**, Queen Mary College, University of London, **Dr Eric Herring**, University of Bristol, **Dr Glen Rangwala**, University of Cambridge, and **Professor Sami Zubaida**, Birkbeck College, University of London; gave evidence.

Q1 Chairman: Good morning. Welcome. This is our first evidence session in a new inquiry into UK operations in Iraq. What we are going to be considering is the political and security situation in Iraq, what are the prospects for national reconciliation and what the progress is on security sector reform and reconstruction and what the future is of the UK Forces in Iraq. We have got a couple of hours this morning. We had to start a bit late—I am sorry about that—because of the queues outside; but welcome to our witnesses. We have got a lot of ground to cover. I wonder if you would begin, please, by introducing yourselves and saying what your background is, very briefly?

Dr Rangwala: I am Dr Glen Rangwala, a Lecturer in politics at Cambridge University and a Fellow at Trinity College, Cambridge. I teach Middle Eastern politics and have been doing research in Iraq over the past four years. I am co-author of a book, *Iraq in Fragments*, with Eric Herring, my neighbour.

Dr Herring: I am Dr Eric Herring. I am Senior Lecturer in International Politics at the University of Bristol, co-author of the book *Iraq in Fragments*, with Glen here, obviously, and, some years previous to that, I have been conducting research into UN sanctions policy on Iraq and so it has been a continuing interest, US, UN, UK policy towards Iraq.

Dr Dodge: I am Dr Toby Dodge. I am a Reader in International Politics at Queen Mary College, University of London, and a Senior Fellow at the International Institute for Strategic Studies. I have worked on Iraq all my academic life, as a political scientist. I was in Baghdad recently, for the month of April, both in the Green Zone and then travelling through Baghdad and down to Mahmudiyah, Latifiyah, Yusufiyah and then finally to Basra.

Professor Zubaida: I am Sami Zubaida. I am Emeritus Professor of Politics and Sociology at Birkbeck College. I work on religion, culture and politics in the Middle East. I was born in Iraq so I have a special interest in Iraq, a comparative perspective, so to speak.

Dr Ansari: I am Dr Ali Ansari. I am a Reader in Modern History at the University of St Andrews and my specialism is actually Iran, so I am here looking at Iran; it is near abroad, I guess.

Q2 Chairman: Thank you very much. Gentlemen, can we start by asking, what are the underlying causes of the violence in Iraq; which are the principal insurgent groups, if insurgent groups are part of the causes of that violence, and what are they trying to achieve? Dr Dodge, you were there last month?

Dr Dodge: I was there during April, trying to assess the success of the surge. I think the cause is the collapse of the Iraqi state; the state was put under 13 years of the worst sanctions ever imposed, I think, in international history. It did what it was meant to do, but at the wrong time, so as too few American troops reached Baghdad they could not control the looting, the civil servants that were running the state had gone through three roles in 20 years and the state was taken to pieces. I was in Baghdad in May 2003 seeing the almost complete destruction of the state. If you add on to that the now infamous decisions to disband the Iraqi Army and to de-Ba'athise, what de-Ba'athification did was take away what was left of the state, the senior levels of the Civil Service, its institutional memory. Into that vacuum firstly stepped criminals and then insurgents fighting to drive out American occupiers, and then, finally, militias, legitimising themselves by sectarian ideology, and that big stew of violence is the Iraqi civil war as it stands. The one thing I would add to that is the complexity of this situation; the final legacy that Saddam Hussein left to the country was, by using vast amounts of violence and money, he combed through society, breaking any organisational capacity he did not control, so the organisations I have just described to you, the militias, the criminals, the insurgents, are deeply fractured and very fluid. The danger would be to simplify the groups on an ethnic or organisational basis, and I do not think any one group has the coherence to be called institutionalised.

Dr Herring: I would agree with all of that and would add a number of things to it. The first is that in different parts of Iraq you have different conflicts and they are certainly not all inter-sectarian. In the west of Iraq there is now a developing conflict between Sunni Arab elements which are connected with the Coalition versus those opposed to it versus those supporting al-Qaeda in Iraq. In the north of Iraq you have the potential struggle over Kirkuk, which obviously is Kurdish Turkoman and Arab. In the south of Iraq, although it is relatively quiet, much of the territory, nevertheless it is an intra-Shi'a political and effectively mafia struggle; so a number of complex struggles there. However, the US Department of Defense's own figures show that, and further consistently so, about 70% of the violence, the attacks are directed at Coalition Forces. There is a lot of uncertainty over that figure, the Iraq Study Group says that there is much, much more violence than that, many more attacks, and so the figures are uncertain. In the Coalition's own assessment, it is very much the primary attacks are directed against the Coalition, and what it raises, of course, is the major policy issue, which I am sure we will come to.

Q3 Chairman: We will. Any other comments on which are the principal groups?

Dr Rangwala: I would add that I think a picture of complete disorder within Iraq today would be inaccurate. A number of the insurgent groups have increasingly formed command structures within them that have shown themselves willing to engage in compromises with groups that are not their ideological bedfellows, and so we have seen over the past year, in particular, a number of different groups that were essentially autonomous insurgent groups engaged in deal-making structures with other insurgent groups. We have seen the formation of the so-called Islamic State of Iraq, in Anbar and in Mosul, and in that respect, at least, there is some sense of there being structures within the insurgency which show themselves willing to engage in negotiations.

Q4 Mr Jenkin: This may seem a strange question, but obviously the targets are very varied, sometimes they are other insurgent groups, sometimes they are Government or Police or Iraqi Army targets, sometimes obviously they are the British and American and Coalition Forces. Against whom is the insurgency campaign directed, what is the agenda behind the various insurgencies; because it is not a so-called Shi'a/Sunni civil war, which is often what it is mischaracterised as, is it?

Professor Zubaida: I think you are quite right, it is not just simply sectarian, or ethnic, I think it is also a battle over resources. In fact, if you look at, for instance, the battles in Basra and in the south of Iraq, it is over control of oil resources, of smuggling gangs; most of the people there, well, all the sides there are Shi'ite but they are divided along different loyalties to different parties, to different tribes, straightforward gangs and mafias, and so on, so I think part of the objectives of the insurgency are actually control of material resources: profit.

Q5 Chairman: Dr Dodge, you looked as though you wanted to answer that question?

Dr Dodge: I just think 'insurgency' is probably the wrong word now, that we have a series of different groups fighting different wars. Glen is right, that there has been some solidification of the insurgency, but that solidification is our next state of Iraq, for example, resulting again in a second splitting, so we have, I think, a series of different groups, some coming together, some splitting. If you were to look at the extrajudicial killings in Baghdad—1,400 in January, 800 in February, 550 in March, 550 in April, 700 in May—that would give you another example of a civil war that is being driven by ethnic cleansing, so what we have is a multi-level conflict. As Eric has said, there are different geographical struggles going on, but I think if you were looking for the overarching explanation for that it is this security vacuum which these different groups have stepped into, with different objectives.

Q6 Chairman: We have got a lot of questions to cover, so although there is much that could be said on this can I ask what is the position now and has it got better or worse in recent months?

Dr Rangwala: The number of multiple-fatality bombings, the number of extrajudicial killings, has gone down in recent months since the injection of new US troops into Baghdad. Therefore, the question arises, to what extent is that a permanent reduction in the violence in Baghdad, in particular, and in the rest of Iraq more generally; is this a situation in which those groups which did engage in those multiple-fatality bombings and extrajudicial killings have been disbanded. I think the answer there has to be pessimistic, that, in some sense, these groups have either left Baghdad and are operating outside the capital city, or have just stored their weapons away temporarily, waiting for the US Forces which are there, going to be there really for only another few months, at current levels, to depart from the country. In that sense, I believe there is a temporary lull in the violence, but not a reduction.

Dr Herring: The US Department of Defense's own figures say that the overall number of deaths globally in Iraq has continued to increase very slightly in this period, and so there is a displacement of violence to other parts of Iraq and a destabilisation of places which were relatively quiet; it is definitely a decline. There are other measures of decline, which would be including increasing support across Iraqi communities, in Shi'a and in some Kurdish elements as well, for attacks on Coalition Forces. Iraqis are now, broadly, evenly divided on this. More Iraqis than ever want Coalition Forces to leave, and support for the idea of an Iraqi national state, while still in a majority, is declining really noticeably, from about 80% into the 50s. There is a fundamental decline; the strategy cannot work, in terms of these kinds of trends. The standing up of Iraqi Forces is not linked to a decline in the killings; they are both on the same upward trajectory.

Q7 Robert Key: Gentlemen, do you think Coalition Forces are still an essential stabilising element, or do they just fuel the violence?

Dr Dodge: I think they are a stabilising force. I think where we have seen them withdraw, especially in the provinces in the south, the violence has increased and there has been a sharp drop-off. Both Eric and Glen are right to suggest they are the target for violence, but there is an awful lot of violence going on outside their remit. On one level they are not reducing the violence across Iraq but I think they are putting a break, albeit a rather malfunctioning one, on the swift movement to civil war.

Professor Zubaida: I agree with that up to a point, but the point is, by staying there, is the stabilisation of the situation permanent or is it the fact that whenever they leave there is going to be a civil war. If they leave now or if they leave in two years' time it could be the same outcome, unless in the meantime, while we are staying, they have effective measures for controlling, reconciling the different sides in the conflict. I am not sure that they are capable of doing that, so it seems to me that they are there stabilising the situation, to some extent, now; whenever they leave the terrors will be unleashed, in any case.

Q8 Robert Key: Do you see that chaos as inevitable, whatever happens?

Professor Zubaida: No; not inevitable. If, in the meantime, there are actually measures to stabilise the situation, successful measures, although I cannot see what they are, then obviously that will be useful. I am sure that Toby will have some answers to this, but, as far as I can see, as soon as the Americans leave there will be a fight between the different sides to consolidate their territory and to consolidate the resources they control.

Dr Rangwala: I would take Professor Zubaida's point a little bit further. It is my sense that deal-making, national reconciliation between different Iraqi groups is actually hindered by the uncertainty about the future of the US presence in Iraq at present. If some sides believe that the US will continue to stay in the country and support, say, for example, those parties currently in government, they see no good reason to make a deal with, say, the insurgent groups which are aiming for that ousting; they see no reason to engage in compromises because they have got the US to fight on their behalf during those struggles. If there becomes increased certainty about what will happen to the US presence in Iraq, whether they will retain a long-term, small presence, whether they will retain an ability to intervene in the country to support the Government, that would enable different Iraqi groups to engage in compromises in a way which they do not at the moment. Therefore, at least, the uncertainty about the future of the US presence is a major factor which is preventing national reconciliation in that way.

Q9 Robert Key: Dr Rangwala, you gave evidence to the Iraq Commission and you said, with Dr Herring, the immediate withdrawal of British Forces from Iraq would be the right decision, as they are doing little of value, attracting increased hostility and suffering losses in support of an approach that has failed?

Dr Rangwala: Yes, because I believe that it is impossible for the US or the UK to have a credible commitment to stay in Iraq indefinitely. I think that would not be seen as a credible promise by the British or American Governments, in that sense. Therefore, if one wants to stabilise Iraq, the best way of showing the Iraqis that the future, essentially, is in their hands and that they have to make a deal between themselves is to withdraw Forces. That is why I have been a proponent, since over the past year, of the need to scale down and eventually eliminate the US military presence.

Q10 Robert Key: This is seen primarily as an Army operation, a land operation. Can I ask you what you think would be the consequences of the United States, Australian and the British Royal Navy withdrawing their Navies from this area, and it might be interesting to have an Iranian perspective on that?

Dr Ansari: An Iranian perspective: I think that Iran's position vis-à-vis the Coalition as a whole can be viewed as dichotomous, there are two different strategies going on in Tehran, at the moment. One if reflected by, really, I suppose, what you would normally call the Civil Service, the Foreign Ministry and the old hands in Government, and the others being perpetrated, or promoted, by the current Government and Mr Ahmadinejad and his allies in the Revolutionary Guard core. I think the latter would very much like to see a withdrawal of Coalition Forces from a whole range of their activities, both in Iraq and in the Persian Gulf, which of course they will emphasise to you is the Persian Gulf and therefore is something that they have a certain right to monitor. I have to say, I think that views in Tehran are divided, I would not say that it is quite so clear, and there are those that actually see the Coalition presence as doing some good, at the very least in directing certainly insurgency activities away from them. I think there is an acknowledgment in Iran that if the Coalition withdrew then a lot of these groups probably would turn their attention on to the Iranians that are around, so there is a lightning-rod activity, facility, going on there as well, at the very least.

Dr Herring: I would like to say, briefly, that the fundamental role of the Coalition Forces is a destabilising one, because it is permitting the intransigence of forces in Baghdad that are not interested in delivering the things that are necessary for national reconciliation, so it is fundamentally destabilising. Then there are particular operations, like the current one in Diyala Province, which are deeply destabilising because they are highly polarising military exercises, which come across to Sunni Arabs in Iraq as essentially anti-Sunni. Then there are other roles, for which actually there is quite widespread support, the idea of peace-keeping and policing, and so on, which Iraqis can support, and that leads to issues of Naval patrolling, and anti-smuggling activities are in a different category. You are dealing with a fundamental, strategic role, then specific military operations which the US is conducting, which are deeply unhelpful and just a repeat of what we have been doing over and over. Then there are these other, more peace-keeping, policing-orientated activities, which would receive widespread support.

Q11 Robert Key: Is the Iraqi Navy capable of protecting Iraq's bialex(?) ports?
Dr Herring: No.
Professor Zubaida: No.
Dr Dodge: The port in Basra is thoroughly penetrated by militias who cream off, in effect, a tax for everything. The Iraqi Navy has little or no role in stopping that. Just to disagree with my two august colleagues, I think what we are involved in doing is second-guessing the rationality of Iraqi actors, and the vast majority of those Iraqi actors, Eric and Glen claim will come to compromise when the Coalition Forces leave, are at the moment the key national figures involved in perpetrating killings and murders. If you want to look at their motivation and their actions, let us look at what they are doing now. The militias, a vast array of them, and forces within the Iraqi Government are perpetrating violence against other Iraqis. My assessment is the same with Eric and Glen, it is speculation from present events that they will increase their deployment of violence, and not decrease it, when troops go home.
Dr Herring: There is actually not a difference between our positions. If you refuse to support these intransigent troops, they might still prefer chaos to compromise; that is certainly the case. The question is are we stabilising by supporting intransigent groups, and the answer has to be, no. How that will then play out, I agree, they might simply say no, and that is why it is important to know a best case, or the idea that if you try to manipulate them in giving military support and dangle carrots and sticks that they will go for that, it might be just simply another agenda that is very localised.

Q12 Mr Borrow: Just in the same area, what I am not clear about is whether the presence of Coalition troops is actually, in a way, allowing violence to take place, because their mere presence perhaps saves the perpetrators from the consequence of that violence. In other words, if the troops were not there, there would be a reaction and there would be more violence towards the perpetrators of violence; but the mere fact that the troops are there is actually encouraging people to take part in violence without suffering the real consequences which would exist were the troops not there. Is there an element of that?
Dr Herring: That is actually what is happening, right now, in Baqubah. As far as I can see, the current offensive, the so-called Iraqi Army offensive, supported by the Americans, could not have happened without the American Army, and it is the kind of operation which simply should not happen, because that population has no intention of submitting to what they will see as Shi'a rule, they are just not going to do it. They might have to back off a little when the Americans are there in large

numbers, but the American military have said, in the last few days, that the Iraqi Army, so-called, Forces cannot hold Baqubah, and so when the Americans leave the insurgents will come back and they will be fighting to regain their territory and the Shi'a forces will simply have to meet that. I would say that is a major destabilising element.

Q13 Mr Jenkin: How much is this cycle of violence psychologically inevitable, after the terrible years of Saddam's oppression and the systematic decapitation of all the natural leadership of society and the settling of old scores, like a sick wound opening up, and it has just got to let all this out, and it is part of the process that Iraq has got to go through? How much of it is just inevitable; however Saddam departed, whatever happened after Saddam, there is going to be some dreadful reckoning?
Professor Zubaida: I think Saddam laid the basis for it but I do not think it was inevitable. In fact, I think what Saddam had done, as you point out and as has been pointed out before, was destroy any basis of social autonomy, social organisation, political organisation in the country, with the result that the only leadership and coherence that were left were those of religion and tribe, and even then these were fractured, reformed. There was no necessity, no inevitability that these divisions would actually lead to violence. I think one of the most important factors which led to the violence was the policy of the Americans when they got there, which was to abolish, as has been said already, the Government and the Army. What do you expect, if you abolish the Government and the Army and you do not put anything in its place? That really is the crucial factor. Saddam may have laid the grounds for it but what actually activated these primordial solidarities into violence, and formed them as well in groups, was the fact that there was no Government and no Police.

Q14 Linda Gilroy: Does the Maliki Government have the capacity and the will to tackle the violence, and, if not, are there ways in which it can be addressed, and what are they?
Dr Dodge: That is the question which I suspect we are all struggling to answer. Let me give you two sides to the answer. One is, through incentivising the Maliki Government, possibly through saying, as there is a head of steam in Washington, "If you do not do X, Y and Z we are going home, or we'll not fund you; we'll withdraw resources," the argument is you could minimise their room for sectarian behaviour, you could reduce their undoubted evidence of the deployment of government services in a sectarian manner; you could do that. That is one side of the argument. The second side of the argument is that we know that ingrained in the Maliki Government, especially in key ministers of state are sectarian actors who are pursuing a sectarian agenda and/or that the Maliki Government is largely irrelevant to what tentative institutions of state, especially the Police and the militias, are actually wreaking havoc in society. I would argue more towards the first, and the second,

incentivising the Maliki Government, on one basis only, that we have got a series of governmental changes, from the CPA to the Alawi Government, to the Jaffri Government, and with each change in government we have seen a massive drop-off of governmental capacity, of incoherence, and whatever, to try to social-engineer another change in a Government which claims at least a democratic mandate will be extremely disrupting. I think we have to work with what we have got and move heaven and earth through, I suspect, an international compact to work with the Maliki Government and try to reform it, or encourage it to reform.

Professor Zubaida: I would largely agree with what Dr Dodge has said. I think that is the case.

Dr Herring: I would add a number of things to that. You are faced with the basic choice of trying to strengthen what is there, and I would actually oppose that. I would say that it is not a coherent actor, it is an alliance, fundamentally, of Kurdish political forces which are doing mostly their own thing, and, broadly speaking, Shi'a fundamentalist forces who control various aspects of the central Iraqi Government in another alliance with the United States, and we see it that way. We will have to look at how you break up that alliance and how you try to find different politics to come out of that, and I do not think that you map out here, the stages that we do that, it will be something we have to respond to in Iraqi political process. What we need to focus on are the key things of how will the coherent actor emerge and why will it seem more to be gained from negotiating than fighting. No-one is really asking those questions clearly enough, and the surge is simply not going to do that, it is not a coherent actor and it gets more from fighting than from compromising, so there is no point in continuing in that road. There is actually some hope in all of this, which is that you can compare the preferences of most Iraqis, and it has been polled very consistently, we could go into some detail but I will stick to a few specifics. In comparison with what is happening at the national level, it is very different. Overwhelmingly, Iraqis reject sectarianism, overwhelmingly, they think it is being forced upon them, overwhelmingly, actually, they favour some kind of Iraqi national government and some kind of Iraqi national presence, and that is true amongst Kurds as well as Shi'ites. It is not the case that they are all broken down in that way. The question is how do we connect that remaining Iraqi national feeling to some kind of political process, rather than balance the Maliki Government, which has no prospect of delivering it.

Q15 Linda Gilroy: To what extent is that tied up with the success, or lack of success, of the Government in tackling the sectarian divide, and what evidence is there that they have even tried to do that?

Dr Rangwala: The Government itself, as Dr Herring was saying, is largely dependent upon one of the Shi'a political parties, the Supreme Council, now for its parliamentary representation; they are the major bloc. That is left within the mainstream of the United Iraqi Alliance. They have an extensive militia, the Badr Brigades, which are involved in sectarian conflict throughout southern Iraq and in parts of Baghdad; so in that respect they are an actor within a sectarian conflict rather than a mediating force between different sectarian groups. At present, the Maliki Government is facing quite a severe challenge in retaining a parliamentary majority, in any case, and one of the parties within the Shi'a alliance has broken away from it. If the Sadr Movement breaks away from that political alliance, they will be a minority in the Parliament, in any case, and there is a very real prospect, over coming months, of Iraq having a minority Government; so, in that respect at least, it will retain a consistent problem of legitimising itself to its own heartlands.

Professor Zubaida: I agree with that. Really, the Maliki Government is a party in the sectarian conflict in Iraq. In many respects, as a Government it is highly ineffective because it has very little capacity, and it is only the fact that insofar as it depends on its own militias or the various bits of the Government depend on their own militias, which of course just adds to the sectarian conflict. I think it is quite right to say that many Iraqis, when asked, would come out against sectarianism, in favour of national unity and a national government, but the national unity and the national government, as they see it, is under their control. Very few people, except some of the Kurds, would want to divide up Iraq; most of the parties who are Arabs want to keep Iraq as a unit but with themselves in control. This applies, of course, especially in relation to the oil resources, which are so vital for any future Iraqi economy; and these are issues upon which it is very difficult to see how people, under present or foreseeable circumstances, could come to agree.

Q16 Linda Gilroy: Do any of you see any prospect of any of the political actors emerging to rise above those sectarian divides?

Dr Herring: Not until the current ones are undermined. It is worth pointing out that the Maliki Government is under a lot of pressure from within its own Islamic Alliance for not doing enough to protect the Shi'a Muslims, so he is actually putting more effort into that one side of things. I do not see that there is any reason to believe that the current actors have any interest in doing that, especially as they are in government, they are being supported, militarily and economically, and running entire government ministries, and able also, with rampant corruption, to pocket vast personal fortunes in this process. They have just no incentive; and what are they going to do, reach out and undermine their own militia base: I just do not see that, I do not see how it can happen.

Dr Dodge: I agree with all that; it is just that when you look at the comparative studies of civil war, civil society, which is what Eric is looking towards, it is going to find it very difficult to organise. It is the people with the guns who rule the streets, so if you are struggling to get your kids in and out of school, struggling to stop your family being murdered or kidnapped, you are not going to join a political party and put yourself on the front line where the men with guns can shoot you. The Government is undoubtedly corrupt and undoubtedly incoherent; factions within the Government undoubtedly are a central player within the civil war. It is just when you look into society, and Eric is exactly right on all the opinion poll data, where is the organisational capacity going to come from to mobilise and overturn what was, and what the politicians in Government claim is, a democratic electoral mandate given from two elections on a referendum in 2005. Those are the two problems. They claim to have a mandate and society is going to find it very difficult to organise against them.

Professor Zubaida: I think the main element of this society, the kind of educated, urban middle classes, they have been targeted particularly and under great attack, and I think one of the really dire consequences of this conflict is the disempowering, and indeed the displacement, of the middle classes. In fact, many of the people who are now refugees, in Jordan and in Syria, are from this group, not to mention the many professionals and business people who have gone to the Gulf or to Europe or America, in the millions. I think, in many respects, this vital element, which could constitute civil society in Iraq, which is genuinely anti-sectarian, which has been the mainstay of Iraq in the 20th century, has been displaced and disempowered, and that is a very grave question.

Q17 Chairman: Dr Herring, in his evidence to the Iraq Commission, Dr Dodge said that he was vehemently against what is quickly becoming the conventional wisdom, which is to pull troops out, run away and hope for the best. If the current Government, the Maliki Government, has been elected via democratic mandate, why do you think that these people, which Professor Zubaida is talking about, might be tempted back to Iraq to form some sort of civil society, if the first thing that you would advise is undermining that democratically-elected Government?

Dr Herring: There are a couple of elements there. The first is, it was certainly elected through a form of democratic process but it was hardly a particularly free process, and it is certainly not representative of what Iraqis have been saying they want. If you were faced with a situation of rampant militia control, complete breakdown of the state, if you were being picked on and potentially murdered, in this country because you were Scottish or Welsh, you would end up engaging in self-protection and backing forces which would protect you. That is not the same as saying that this is representative of what the people want in Iraq and I am not suggesting that simply by pulling out forces therefore that will emerge. I cannot see how actively supporting, and I will give you a specific illustration, military offences by what is effectively perceived by Sunni Arabs as a Shi 'a occupation force in Diyala Province, that advances, in any way, anyone's rights, regardless of which way they did or did not vote. That is just not the way to go. It is not simply, as I say, a question of leaving or staying, it is a question of what function you play

and what role you play and Iraqis are more interested in that more supportive role. It is not a question of simply leaving and washing your hands, I have never said that.

Dr Rangwala: Just to respond to the very specific point, what will bring the educated professional classes back from Jordan and Syria, what will bring them back is not necessarily a democratic government being in place but a peaceful country, and what will bring a peaceful country is what we have been discussing. My sense is that a number of these groups, which are engaged in quite explicit violence on a very high scale within Iraq, already through back channels have negotiated with each other, they have shown already their willingness to engage in deal-making, and therefore we need to set the conditions in which they can actually implement the very deals which they have drawn up in private already.

Q18 Mr Jenkin: On the back of that question, is not the rather idealised democratic constitution, attempting to base itself on the reconciliation of all the various factions, really misconceived, for the present circumstance? Should we not encourage them to adopt an emergency constitution which is going to allow perhaps a single individual to impose much more control than is possible with a minority government, which is one prospect?

Dr Herring: What you need is coherent actors and there are going to be a number of them in Iraq; there just is not going to be one. That would be magicking someone out of the air to do it. There is no-one who could play that role, there is no-one who would be accepted, they would simply be fought. We have someone in that role; it is called the Coalition, and you are not going to find an Iraqi to do that role. What you need is not just, of course, fluffy civil society, actually you need a military balance in Iraq, an emergent set of forces which made it clear, in western Iraq, "You cannot conquer western Iraq, so stop trying." As long as the Coalition is going to keep on trying to conquer western Iraq they are going to fail to do so; and are they going to back the Government in Baghdad indefinitely, trying to conquer western Iraq? As soon as the Coalition does not back that attempt at conquest, that attempt at conquest will have to stop; and if that becomes part of the emergent forces, in terms of strength, and I think you do have to look at strength as well as civil society, so it is a balance of those coherent political actors and the military situation on the ground.

Q19 Mr Jenkins: Running an army is expensive and running a militia is expensive, and whilst you have a territory of very poor people there is only so much you can squeeze out of poor people. Who exactly is funding these militias?

Dr Herring: They are smuggling oil.

Dr Rangwala: The oil-smuggling, essentially. All the political parties in the south engage in extensive siphoning off of the oil or smuggling of the oil across borders, and in that respect, at least, they get a very large proportion of their income and very extensive amounts of funds from dealing with Iraq's most valuable natural resource: oil.

Dr Herring: Also the United States, all the money it has poured into Iraq, vast volumes of that have just been disappearing, left, right and centre. To give you a specific illustration of how ludicrous the current situation is, an Iraqi soldier gets about $317 a month, the Police get about $50 or $60; they are being issued with $1,000 pistols which they can sell on the black market, and only a tiny proportion of those, or even I think the US do not even bother to take a note of the serial numbers to keep track of those, and this is according to the US's own official figures. If you want to fund your insurgency join the Iraqi Army or join the Police; they are what Glen and I call embedded insurgents. You get a wage for doing it, you get nice, expensive weapons which you can sell on, or just use during the evenings, and then you go back to work in the morning, if you bother to show up. The US official figures say "These are the Iraqi security forces," little asterisk, and down at the bottom it says, "Just by the way, we don't know how many of these people actually show up."

Q20 Mr Hamilton: I am thinking, Chairman, of an 18-month period when the American elections are going to be coming up, so my question to both Glen and Eric is that you do not say you disagree with Toby, in actual fact, what you are really saying is just let the cards fall, withdraw and that will take care of itself, because that is what will happen, in two years' time, three years' time, four years' time. I just want to be clear that is what you are really saying, is it not?

Dr Rangwala: Not really. I think one does not give incentives to Iraqi political parties to make a deal between themselves, but one thing that the British and Americans can do is try to negotiate with the surrounding actors, with the regional states, Iran, Syria, Jordan and Saudi Arabia, to ensure they do not use Iraqi political groups as their own proxies in a turf war in Iraq. I think the main role of the Coalition has to be in ensuring that the regional states do not engage in a way that they could do, with devastating consequences for Iraq if they do.

Dr Herring: Again, I do not say just walk away and wash your hands, but, for example, are you going to try to conquer insurgents by force; the answer simply has to be no, because they have massive support. Are you going to try to conquer the Sadrists by force, as is happening currently, right now; you cannot, so do not try. You must negotiate with them. Engaging all the surrounding actors is a good idea, in the sense that what you must do is you have to do it seriously, not like the United States does currently, where it just wants to get what it can but fundamentally it does not accept your legitimacy. Really, it is going to be an Iraqi national process, because Iraqi nationalism will not be too keen on the idea of the surrounding states, somehow or other, just deciding the future. We will not just walk away, but you have to calculate what will produce coherent actors and what will produce a military balance conducive to negotiations. You cannot win by force and the Coalition should stop trying to do so; it cannot do it.

Q21 John Smith: Do you envisage any strategic threats from the premature withdrawal of the Coalition; strategic threats to the west and to this country in particular?

Dr Dodge: Yes, I do. We have a failed state at the moment which no-one controls; a multi-layered civil war. I think Eric talked about a military balance; what would a military balance look like, as we go forward? I do not think it will look like a neatly-divided Iraq into three areas. Because all of these militias were set up after regime change, bar the two Kurdish militias, they are prepared to come back into a country, and no one group will win and you will have intra-communal and inter-communal war, so you will have a failed state with comparative stability in fractured areas. That looks to me broadly comparable to Afghanistan before the rise of the Taliban. The international community turns its back on a country, the country then descends into civil war with proxies increasingly fighting their own state policies on Iraqi soil. A failed state, already with a rising Islamic radicalism and a transnational Jihadist trend in it, looks to me to pose a distinct threat because it sits on the edge of Europe.

Dr Herring: That is what we have now, but we have layered on top of that Coalition Forces trying to win offensives against two major actors, and that is the absurdity of it. This is the direction we have already; we are already there, it exists. The comparative stability in Basra is precisely because the militias have managed to dominate.

Dr Dodge: There is no stability in Basra.

Dr Herring: Actually, stability in terms of a fragile balance between militias. I do not mean in any positive sense. I think we can agree on that.

Chairman: We are now aware of the general views that you have expressed about Iraq as a whole. Moving on, and dealing first with the surge, David Borrow.

Q22 Mr Borrow: On that point, how successful has the US surge been; is it delivering the results that were expected and what do you expect General Petraeus to report in September?

Dr Dodge: I was travelling through Baghdad in April, which was about the third month of the surge, and travelling on the western bank of the Tigris, Yarmouk, Mansour, what are generally considered Sunni neighbourhoods. You could say, to some extent, in those neighbourhoods, what the surge has done is stopped the militia of the Mahdi Army, Muqtada al-Sadr's militia, coming in and purging those communities of Sunnis, which it did at least for 12 months. To a certain extent, we have seen somewhat of a drop-off in extrajudicial killings, but, as Eric was saying, that is an incredibly localised and probably temporary issue and that has led directly to the fighters, the militias and insurgents, moving out of the capital to Diyala, where violence has increased massively. On that level, I do not think the surge has yet been successful. Secondly, in my wildest imagination I cannot see General Petraeus turning up at Congress in September and saying "It's all over; let's go home." What he will say is "Here is the data; I think we need more time." That is crystal-ball-gazing, or anyway controversial; he will try to push for more time.

Dr Herring: Briefly, it is a blip not a surge, in the sense that there is a small increase in Forces to below the maximum previously there, so actually you could call this the refusal to go back to previous levels, the maintained cut, would be just as accurate a description. Presumably we will be going to get on to political benchmarks because the surge was meant to create the space for the achievement of the political benchmarks on provincial elections, the reversal of some de-Ba'athification, compromising on the Constitution, oil revenue-sharing and the future of the oil industry. All of that, more or less, is struggling very much, and effectively I think has stalled, even the things that they claimed to have some agreement on, so the idea of surge to create some political space has failed.

Q23 Mr Borrow: There has been some talk about the approach of the UK as opposed to the US; at the same time as the US is putting extra troops into the surge the UK is drawing down troops from the south. Do they represent different strategies or are they part of a single strategy, and what has been the reaction in the south to the draw-down of the UK Forces?

Dr Rangwala: There has been a consistently different strategy taken by the British in the southern governance, in the south-east of Iraq, from the US approach in central Iraq, essentially. The British approach has been a much more hands-off approach; in that sense, they have not tried to intervene in many of the disputes that have taken place between the different groups within Basra, they have not tried to intervene in some areas in which they know that they will provoke a violent response. This is quite different from the US approach, which is essentially tackling those areas, sending their troops into those areas in order to impose a new form of rule in those towns or cities concerned. The British approach at the moment of scaling down its presence to 5,500 troops in Basra essentially is a continuation of that hands-off approach. We are likely to see the removal of British Forces from their central base in Basra completely over the coming months, and I think, in that sense, at least, it is part of that different approach that the British have taken.

Q24 Mr Jenkin: Is not really the future of Iraq dependent upon the politics of Washington, rather than the merits of any particular strategy or policy any General or department in Washington might adopt?

Professor Zubaida: I think there are many issues in Iraq which are dependent upon policy in Washington, but given that Washington has proved to be so impotent in actually managing Iraq then there must be very limited issues which are determined by Washington. I think one of the big questions that will be determined by Washington is the future of the Kurdish region. In fact, the Kurdish region is relatively well-off, relatively stable, and so

on, but that depends very much on continued American support and keeping Turkish Forces at bay. That is one of the issues which depend very much on Washington and what happens in the future. Given that Washington has not really been terribly successful in controlling Iraq, I do not know, apart from the decision to stay or withdraw, and in what form to stay, there are so many elements in Iraq, as has been made very clear, which are not under control.

Dr Ansari: I just want to add, I think that the situation in Iraq, in the border region, could probably be, in some ways, certainly affected perhaps in a positive way if US policy towards the region was a little bit more coherent. I am focusing particularly on Iran there.

Q25 Mr Jenkin: Lots of people talk about engaging Iran. How should we do that and what are we trying to achieve?

Dr Ansari: My own view is that you are not going to get broader results in the war on terror, be it Afghanistan or Iraq, unless you begin to have some sort of coherent policy and strategy towards Iran. Engagement can mean a broad range of issues. At the moment, as far as I can see, the United States and Iran are settling into a rather uneasy war of attrition and some of the excesses of this war of attrition are being seen in Afghanistan and Iraq. On the one hand, the Americans are pushing for a fairly tight and, I would say, in some ways, quite successful economic embargo, in a sense, a sort of siege of the Iranian economy, which is beginning to bite, and the Iranians are beginning to retaliate by supporting a whole range of different proxy groups, to try to put pressure on the Coalition. I have to say that we generalise at our peril, in a sense, because clearly in the United States as well there are some strong divisions within the Administration as to how to proceed. On my recent trip to the United States, I was quite struck to see the differences in opinion between the State Department and, say, for instance, the Vice President's Office. The Vice President's Office seemed to be carrying on a policy, quite distinct and of its own, as far as, say, Baluchistan was concerned. There are things going on which I do not think are terribly helpful, but you can see how the Iranians might retaliate in kind by supporting units like the Taliban or supporting even Sunni insurgents in Iraq, however limited I consider those to be, but nonetheless obviously it exists.

Q26 Mr Jenkin: The West is torn between a policy which might be characterised as carpets and pistachios and being nice to the trading ruling class in Iran, or carrier groups and backing the PMI. Should we be doing either of those two things, or both of them; are they mutually exclusive?

Dr Ansari: In my view, I think the latter point is probably not helpful. I do not think it is helpful at all to be backing groups such as the PMI, principally because until they can convince me that they are a democratic opposition I do not see what the point of them is. On the other hand, yes, there are elements, and one of the things we find in Iran is that it is a very plural political system, that there are options for engagement with different groups. The problem with western policy, I think, towards Iran is it has been too monolithic, so we fail to see the distinctions between different groups, we tend, as you say, to have carpets and pistachios, in a general sense, in a sense mollifying even the more hard-line elements. The great joke in Iran today is that when we had a President who talked about dialogue with civilisations we responded with the axis of evil and when we have a President who talks about the Holocaust we offer him talks. This is the thing, that there is sort of a contradiction in western policy, and particularly coming out of Washington, and it is not missed in Iran, the Iranians see it. Even Iranians who have no affection whatsoever for Mr Ahmadinejad are struck by the fact that he seems to get away with murder, and they wonder what his magic is, his great trick is, really. What they do not understand is, and this is, as I am sure you appreciate, as far as Britain is concerned, they certainly cannot conceive that anything that Britain does is anything but calculated at the most profound level. The notion that Britain might in some ways make a mistake, or not actually deal with something in a coherent manner, is inconceivable to most Iranians because that is simply not the way Britain works.

Q27 Mr Jenkin: What sort of Iraq does Iran legitimately want and how do we appeal to Iran's legitimate interests?

Dr Ansari: I was struck by one of the comments that Sami made earlier. We have this situation of various different groups which all want a united Iraq but no-one can be in control of it. I think the Iranians can be counted as one of those groups which want a united Iraq but want to be in control of it. Ultimately, they see themselves as being there when the Coalition has gone. They have a certain complacency about it, of course, they consider themselves to have been around for thousands of years and will continue to be so and they see Iraq as their justifiable near abroad, as I used the term earlier. I think, by and large, the comments that were made to me certainly, and this is, I have to say, a while back, certainly 18 months to two years ago, but when I was talking to some senior officials their argument was very strongly in favour of a united Iraq but a united Iraq which was militarily weak. Their red line was "We will not allow, at any stage, a military threat to emerge from this country again. That is our red line. What emerges out of Iraq, out of that, ideally, we would like a politically unified Iraq, one that can be a good market for Iranian goods." This is the sort of thing that they are looking at. If the country was to fragment, they think they can manage it, with the Turks, and that is their view.

Q28 Mr Jenkin: Moving on, we know that lots of stuff comes over the border, which is killing our soldiers, bluntly; is this with the support, the permission, the active involvement of the Iranian Government?

Dr Ansari: I think that there is a dual layer in Government in Iran, since 2004 this has been particularly evident; one is basically what you would call the orthodox republican elements of government machinery, and the other is the IRGC, and the IRGC, the Islamic Revolutionary Guard Corps, tends to operate on its own agenda. I think, where you find some of the more unhelpful elements of Iranian intervention in Iraq, it comes from the IRGC. Their response, incidentally, will be "This is our response" to what they perceive to be US/British intervention in Khuzistan or in Baluchistan. There is a cycle of violence emerging, which I suspect is part of the whole fragmentation of political life in Iraq, which is spilling over the border; but that is the way they see it. There are other ideological agendas going on, of course, where they say "We want to make life as uncomfortable as possible," for two different reasons. One is "If the Coalition is kept busy they won't pay attention to us;" and, two, "Perhaps we can encourage them to leave earlier," because some of them believe that Iran will be in a very strong position to be the dominant player. I think there are others, of course, in the Foreign Ministry and other cases, many of whom are not in Government actually at the moment, who would argue that both views are fanciful, that actually there should be some sort of constructive engagement with the Coalition, tacitly, behind the scenes, you would never say it publicly, of course, to ensure that some form of stable Iraq is left, because the last thing they want is, as Toby drew the analogy, another Afghanistan on their western border.

Q29 Mr Jenkin: If we got the support of the Iranian Government, could they actually stop the flow of weaponry across the border?

Dr Ansari: Inasmuch as there is IRGC intervention then, yes, that could be stopped. I do not think there is a problem there. Inasmuch as there are entrepreneurial elements at work, that is more difficult, yes.

Q30 Mr Jenkin: The Committee was recently briefed on the Fulton Report into the capture of the UK Naval personnel. One of the questions we were asking was what was the motive behind this attack? What do you think was in the minds of IRGC; was it their idea, was it somebody else's idea, was it a local thing? What was behind it?

Dr Ansari: I think the IRGC had made it quite clear that they wanted to retaliate for the seizure of the Irbil Five; the intelligence was there.

Q31 Mr Jenkin: The intelligence was there: that is a very serious accusation to make?

Dr Ansari: It was on their website; they were making announcements about it, they were saying "We will go after blonde, blue-eyed . . . " What they did not say, necessarily, was "We will go after a British Naval vessel." The assumption was they would target the Americans. My view of that is, judging from the experience of 2004, if they were going to go after people probably they would not go after Americans. There was always vulnerability there, but the fact is that, on the occasion of the Persian New Year, the Supreme Leader, Ayatollah Khomeini, effectively gave the go-ahead. He said, in his speech, very clearly, that "If the Coalition persists in illegal activities, we will retaliate with illegal activities of our own."

Q32 Mr Jenkin: Does that include the capture of the Irbil Five?

Dr Ansari: The Irbil Five was a factor; it was them plus there was a defection, supposedly, of an Iranian Minister of Defence, there were also the diplomats which were being abducted. We have to bear in mind that from the moment that George W Bush announced, I think it was, in January, or December, I cannot remember, that Iranian personnel would be legitimate targets of Coalition Forces, and you have this sudden surge—splurge—whatever, seeking to abduct as many Iranians as you can in Iraq, to curtail their activities, the likelihood of a retaliation was always there, and they made it very clear. The Irbil Five, despite the fact, of course, that the Iranians, during the whole episode of the sailors, officially would say "There is no link," very frequently, when you got to point two, the link became very apparent, the link was there. They wanted, first of all, access to the individuals, there was no access; as usual, the individuals were abducted, there was no Red Cross access, there was no diplomatic access, they did not know where they were. I think now we have Red Cross access. As I understand it, from Tehran, there was an assumption, they were led to believe, now whether this is true or not I have no idea of saying, that they would be released on the occasion of the Persian New Year, and when they were not released on the occasion of the Persian New Year I think the go-ahead was given that they should act.

Mr Jenkin: You would think it entirely reasonable for HMS Cornwall's Intelligence Officer to have been furnished with or to have access to that kind of intelligence?

Chairman: That is not a question for Dr Ansari.

Q33 Mr Jenkins: What exactly is the relationship between Iran and Russia at the present time; how close are they?

Dr Ansari: I think one of the unfortunate consequences of the developments in Iranian politics that you are seeing now is part of a tighter relationship with Russia. As you see Mr Putin going down the route of growing autocracy, I think you can see his influences reigning large in Iran at the moment. There is a very strong business link, basically, between the two; black market links, I suppose, is the polite way of putting it. It is very strong business links, and so on. I think also, from the Russian perspective, they see the issue of Iran as a useful stick with which to beat the United States. It is leverage for the Russians, as far as I can see. It is the old game.

Mr Jenkins: Yes, it is the great game returns.

Chairman: Dr Ansari has been talking about Iran at some length and very helpfully. Is there anything any of you would like to add to that, or would you like to bask in his wisdom: right, then let us move on.

Mr Jenkins: Thank you very much. That is very helpful.

Q34 Willie Rennie: To what extent is there a risk that the sectarian violence in Iraq could spill over to a regional war, with the Sunnis and Shi'as?

Dr Dodge: I think, if this is King Abdullah of Jordan's rather ill-measured and extreme statements about the crescent of crisis, and maybe King Adbullah can say that because he has no indigenous Shi'a population of his own, a spill-over into a regional war is highly unlikely; extremely unlikely. I think what is much more likely is that conflict will be contained in Iraq and regional tensions will be fought out in Iraq by proxy. I think there is a great deal of very realistic worry in Saudi Arabia and in Jordan that they are living on the edge of a failed state and that what they want to do is seal their borders and push the conflict away from them. Their big fear is, as US troops draw down and as the situation gets worse, there will be less and less to stop the regional players playing in and we will get, basically, a cold war, a proxy war, between Iran and Saudi Arabia in Iraq. That, I would argue, would have nothing to do with sectarian identity; that would be dressed up as sectarian identity. It would be reasons of state, the two ruling élites fighting each other across the dead bodies of the Iraqis.

Professor Zubaida: There is also very strong Sunni Salafi sentiment in Saudi Arabia and that Saudi influence around the world against the Shi'a, and this translates often into internal conflicts within these countries, so, in fact, with the Iraq situation, the Shi'a of Saudi Arabia have come under greater pressure and the tensions between Shi'a and Sunni in Bahrain have been sharpened, as a result of Iraq. In fact, there is a certain degree of triumphalism of oppressed Shi'a minorities in Saudi Arabia and some of the Gulf States, through the Iraqi Shi'a resurgence; this, of course, is also true in Pakistan. In fact, while I agree with Toby that it will not lead to a regional war, possibly greater intervention by proxy within Iraq, at the same time I think we have to look at the internal situation in many of these countries, which have a significant Shi'ite community.

Dr Herring: You do get pockets of local fighting and balancing and settling-up, and there has been no reference to Basra; what you have there is the dominance of militia forces which have driven people out. They killed off the former Ba'thists, they killed off the local intelligentsia, the dominant local tribes, and they established something that they managed to settle themselves, very violently and with lower levels of continuing violence. Surrounding states will not look to just throw themselves, willy-nilly, into doing their own fighting and trying to work out all of this locally; they do have these incentives to continue and extend the involvement, and picking horses rather than going in themselves.

Dr Dodge: Let me give you an example. Basra is quite fascinating; the extent to which the powers in Basra have been picked, or created, by Iranian funding is a matter for discussion.

Professor Zubaida: I think, in speaking of Basra, there are also other parts; we have forgotten about the Christians. In fact, one of the sectors of victims of this situation has been the smaller Christian communities in Iraq. Whereas all the official political leaders and religious leaders make noises about tolerance and unity, and what have you, the actual facts on the ground, of the militias and the various groups which try to force their authority over neighbourhoods and communities, have been that the Christians have been targeted. In many ways, they have been, in some areas, and I think in Basra, particularly, under great pressure and some have been ethnically cleansed, so to speak.

Q35 Willie Rennie: We have touched on this issue briefly already, about dialogue with Iran, not so much about Syria, but do you think there is really constructive dialogue or do you think it is tokenistic, between the US, UK and all the various states?

Dr Herring: From what I have seen, it appears fundamentally to be token; primarily because the United States is extremely hostile to those states. There might be tactical accommodations they can both make and so they can actually get real deals on some specifics, but it does not change the fact that when you spend time in the United States, for example, in the case of Iran daily, the American media is awash with just an amazing amount of hostile material, being over there. You have all the stuff on television about how the Iranians are going round the New York Subway system, taking down all the targets that they can use for their possible chemical weapons and nerve gas in the US Subway. That kind of frenzied mentality in the United States is not conducive to serious engagement. There has to be a choice; are you even going to recognise the Iranian state, are you going to establish full diplomatic relations, are you going to deal with it as a legitimate state, or not, and if they cannot fundamentally bring themselves to do that then it is hardly surprising if those states are not going to co-operate fully in your regional designs.

Q36 Willie Rennie: Do you think that applies to Syria as well?

Dr Herring: Less so, but it is still fundamentally yes.

Professor Zubaida: I think, when we talk about engaging with, the question really is what are you going to give them; presumably engaging with means negotiating: what are you going to negotiate, what are you going to offer? Syria has a whole list of objectives, in relation to Israel, the region, Lebanon, what have you; what lines are you going to follow with this, for instance? The other question to ask is, supposing you did get Syria on your side, what can Syria do, what can they achieve; apart from closing their borders and stopping the Iraqi exiles being active there, or whatever, really there is very little they can do in terms of controlling the situation in Iraq.

Dr Rangwala: I think there are very specific things which can be achieved through negotiation with Iran, in the short term. Border liaison and co-operation over the border and naval liaison are two of those things which can be achieved through negotiation, and are achievable. Both have been attempted in the past by the British, actually, the British Ambassador in Iraq entered into negotiations with both Syria and Iran, with regard to stabilising the border region and co-operating over that, as well as, I believe, over naval liaison, in 2004. Both were called off by the opposing side, as it were, Syria and Iran, as US rhetoric against both those countries escalated. In that context, at least, a more subdued US critical tone towards those two countries will enable those short-term objectives to be secured, with respect to Iraq.

Dr Ansari: There are two things I want to talk about. One is, the difficulty we find with Iran, of course, is you have a Government which does not want to talk; that makes it more difficult, obviously, and I do not want to romanticise the prospects of having a good dialogue with Iran at present. At the same time, I would want to say that I think the problem with western, American policy in particular to Iran is that I simply do not think Iran really, for the last 30 years, has been taken seriously enough at high levels of political decision-making. The sad thing is that Iran is seen very much as an aspect of another problem, so we either talk to Iran as part of the Iraqi problem, the Afghan problem, any other problem, and we fail to look at Iran just on its own merits and its own particularities. Until we do that we are not going to get results; it is just simply not going to happen.

Q37 Willie Rennie: What about the Arab-Israeli conflict, peace process, what kind of an effect is that having on Iraq and the region as a whole?

Dr Herring: There is a very widespread commentary that you find just about everywhere that really you cannot make progress on Iraq until you take seriously the Arab-Israeli problems. I would dispute that, pretty fundamentally. What is happening in Iraq is actually very Iraqi and I think it would really help if we took the substance from Ali's point, that we take Iraq and what is happening there more seriously. Rather than having the recent lurch towards referring obsessively to al-Qaeda in Iraq, every time something happens it is al-Qaeda, it is not even al-Qaeda in the Mesopotamia region, it is the Iraqi version of it, it is actually simply al-Qaeda, it is incredibly unhelpful and also the references to Iran, and therefore they are implying that everything in Iraq is to do with everything else except Iraq. This, again, is part of the problem, I would suggest, and what happens in Iraq can be de-linked from the Arab-Israeli conflict, that is not what they are fighting about.

Dr Rangwala: Fundamentally, I agree with that. I think, especially in southern Iraq, the battles are essentially local battles being fought by different parties, all of them drawing, to some extent, upon Iranian support to some degree, but they are local battles and have their own dynamics, quite independently of external actors. Whether that be actors involved in the Arab-Israeli conflict or engaged in struggles between the US and Iran at present, they are local battles which can be resolved on their terms.

Q38 Chairman: Drawing on Iranian support to some degree; is there evidence of Iranian manufacture of IEDs and of Iranian training of insurgents in Iraq?
Professor Zubaida: I think one point is worth making, which is not a direct answer to your question, which is that for the most part the Americans and the Iranians are supporting the same side in Iraq; that, in fact, the main Iranian client in Iraq is SCIRI, the Supreme Council for the Islamic Revolution in Iraq, and they are precisely the main ingredient in the Maliki Government, which is supported by the United States. The idea that somehow Iran is arming the other side against the United States may be correct to a very small extent, but the main thrust of Iranian influence and Iranian support in Iraq is the same side as that of the United States. I think that is worth keeping in mind.

Q39 Chairman: What a curious business.
Dr Rangwala: I would disagree with that slightly. My sense is that the Iranians are backing every side, they are backing every horse in the race, as it were, within Iraq at present, they are backing groups which are opposed to the Supreme Council as well as backing the Supreme Council itself, so that no group takes— -
Professor Zubaida: Are they backing Sunni insurgents though?
Dr Rangwala: I think they are, as well. They have shown in the past their willingness to support groups which are fundamentally ideologically opposed to Iran, in the hope that will bring them into a position of a *modus vivendi* with Iran over other issues.

Q40 Chairman: Specifically, are they exporting IEDs, or exporting the expertise?
Dr Herring: The information which has been made available in the public domain by the United States on this is inconclusive at best.

Q41 Chairman: You cannot make it conclusive in front of us?
Dr Herring: There has been nothing that I have seen, in terms of all the claims about serial numbers and manufacture, and so on, nothing enough for me to say, yes, I have seen that. Also, the fundamental thing is, if you are worried about weapons coming over the border, they are coming in via the United States. There is no shortage of weapons in Iraq, they do not particularly need them from Iran, and that is a critical factor; so they are important politically but trivial militarily.

Q42 Chairman: Are relations improving between local government in Basra Province and the United Kingdom Armed Forces?
Dr Dodge: Do you mean specifically Governor al-Waili?

Q43 Chairman: Let us start with him, yes.
Dr Dodge: Certainly he is a frequent visitor to the Airport and he has long and detailed discussions with British diplomatic and military representation there. I would go as far as to say that I would not think the British support him, and I would hope they would not, because one would have deep misgivings about his style and approach to government. They have gone up and down, certainly during Operation Sinbad, and then the targeting, the brief, more forward-leaning forage of the British military into Basra, relations went down, depending if the British tripped across militias around Fadullah, the party which supports the Government. At the moment, the Governor's own political position is very weak, so I suspect he is looking to the British for some kind of sustenance, and not receiving it, as far as I know.

Q44 Chairman: We have heard already all you have said about the general position of the Coalition Forces, but how are UK Forces in the south-east regarded and, subject to what you have said, are they a contribution to stability or are they destabilising?
Dr Rangwala: I spent some time with Basrawi academics in Jordan last week, and their fundamental position seemed to be that British Forces were actually irrelevant to much of what goes on within Basra, they rarely saw them, they rarely engaged with any British institutions, and in that respect they have marginalised themselves from the politics and society of Basra. They have not taken on the sort of role which is either stabilising or destabilising, in that sense, within the city.

Q45 Willie Rennie: Is that a good thing or a bad thing, do you think?
Dr Rangwala: It is an irrelevant thing; not a good thing or a bad thing, I suppose.

Q46 Mr Holloway: What do people think the British are for then, in southern Iraq?
Dr Dodge: I think two things. I would not disagree with Glen that they are just about to give up their base in town, they are hunkered down at the Airport, they are getting mortared at the Airport, more I suspect to put pressure on London than anything else; that is all true. However, I suspect, in the highly unstable and extremely violent arena that Basra in politics is, a complete withdrawal of the British may trigger, may destabilise and increase the violence there. I do not know if that is true or not but that would be something to put on the table; their presence limited but there is some ill-fitting brake on the violence.

Q47 Mr Holloway: Can I ask the Professor, so they are not there for anything, they are there just in case?
Professor Zubaida: I take the view, as I said earlier about the Coalition Forces in general, that Toby may be right that, in fact, they are a brake on much wider violence, but the question is how long can they stay and be a brake and, if they do not leave now, at any time in the future when they leave will the

situation be any better, is the question. Of course, it depends what can be done in the meantime, and I am not sure what can be done in the meantime.

Q48 Mr Holloway: I do not know if this is a fair characterisation of what you seem to be saying, Professor, but are you suggesting really that it is time now for us to get out and let Iraq get on with its civil war? If that is the case, do other people agree?

Professor Zubaida: I would really hesitate to suggest anything, certainly anything—it is such a desperate situation—which might increase the violence would be irresponsible to advocate. At the same time, this is a genuine question that I am posing, if they were to stay there and leave in two years' time, what is going to happen in these two years which is going to lead to a different outcome? This is really a question that I cannot answer.

Dr Rangwala: My sense in Basra is that the Fadilah Party runs the oil protection force, the Supreme Council run the Intelligence Services, the Sadr Party run much of the Police Force in Basra, and in that sense, at least, the British presence does not have a significant impact upon those different relations between those different parties, each running different sectors of the Basra Armed Forces.

Q49 Mr Holloway: Should we leave and let them get on with the civil war?

Dr Rangwala: I do not think there is a civil war and I do not think there is in Basra specifically, and I do not think that there is an impact upon the low-level violence which continues to occur between different armed groups within Basra itself.

Dr Dodge: I think it is simply, periodically, outright conflict breaks out and violence flows. I think to qualify that as low level is simply not the case. People are dying in Basra. Basra is a lawless place where the politics of the gun dominate; that is not low-level violence, that is anarchy, and it could get worse or it could stay at a steady state.

Q50 Mr Hamilton: Surely, Chairman, the point that Dr Rangwala is making is that the Brits are not involved in all that; they have stepped back out of that, and therefore why should they be there? It seems to me there is a difference of opinion in relation to how best we deal with a diverse Iraq. What is happening in the north is not the same as what is happening in the south and the reactions are different. The real question, because there is a difference and I do not want to go away from here with a difference of opinion, not being fair myself, effectively, you are saying, as I understand it, the Brits could walk out tomorrow and it would not make much difference at all in the south, and the real question is why are we there then?

Dr Herring: There are a couple of things in that. It varies from place to place and if you take Maysan Province, in which the British Forces have been fighting recently, and so have the American Forces, the irony is that the British military's own opinion-polling shows that the vast majority of the population support attacks on British Forces, that is the British military's own internal polling; whereas

only a minority in Basra support attacks on British Forces. Again, you have to look at what they are doing. What people locally would like is British Forces to help, occasionally they do take on militiamen, they do actually free people who have been tortured, and so on, and that has got to be a good thing, but it is not going to fundamentally reshape the politics of that area and sometimes it is just going to escalate, especially whenever you are involved with the American anti-Sadr agenda, which is just not going to work there. You cannot defeat any of these people this way, even if you do help things occasionally, and, Toby is right, you will simply get major outbreaks of fighting as they try to rebalance against themselves; but that is happening anyway again.

Q51 Mr Hamilton: I am waiting to hear what Dr Dodge will say, because your view seems to be they are better there in case a major problem comes and they are already there. That is not the same thing as your two colleagues; your two colleagues basically are telling us "Let's go home because we're doing nothing there anyway"?

Dr Dodge: No. There is a difference of interpretation about what the future holds. I do not think we are disagreeing particularly on the hell that Iraq is in, and I have not got a solution. I think the solution that they will be forced to come to an accommodation when the Coalition Forces pull out is fundamentally mistaken, but that is a little bit of a disagreement between us. What I would say is, we are in the midst of a civil war, when the US and the UK pull out, and ironically I think they will pull out, I just do not think they should, the chances of a re-intervention are next to nothing. It is a very low justification for Coalition troops continuing to be there; once they have gone there is no solution. While they are there, there may be the possibility of a solution; and, just to add, if there is a multilateral solution with the UN it certainly will not come about once the US has gone home.

Dr Herring: This is a critical point, because really I think we are getting to the nub of the whole thing, in relation to the UK presence there. The first thing is, British Forces are dying, about one a week, on average, and really we have to have a better reason for that than, vaguely, "We might sometimes help," and I would argue that sometimes we do. Glen and I have never said we are sure that these people will be forced to an accommodation upon its departure, especially not in the south; they have already, mostly, got their own accommodations and then they decide not to have them and they fight. Sometimes Britain, and you are right, happens to just stumble across one particular militia group and the Governor happens to be happy. That is just no way to continue to have British Forces killed. Whether or not you have a re-intervention, that is not a reason to stay in a bad situation, just because you will not go back there. This is not something that we are capable of solving. British Forces cannot resolve it, which is why lives are being lost, pretty needlessly, even if occasionally they help on something; and things may get worse in the short term, but that is not a reason. They are going to go anyway so there are just going to be more people dying; more British Forces die, then they go. That is an even worse outcome.

Q52 Chairman: You are not saying that things would get better if we left; you are saying that things have no chance of getting better while we are there, is that right?

Dr Herring: It may be that, incidentally, things happen to turn out to get better, but we will not be causing that, we will not fundamentally be causing that; that is just beyond British control. We are not involved to a degree that would possibly deliver that kind of control.

Q53 Mr Holloway: What is the use of staying then, if there is no plan and we do not really understand why we are there any more?

Dr Dodge: There is a plan. It is being executed by General David Petraeus.

Q54 Mr Holloway: Yes, but the British?

Dr Dodge: I assume, I would not want to speak for our new Prime Minister but there are two things, that there is a great deal of resentment in Washington and in the American Embassy in Baghdad at the draw-down discussion, and I think that was handled very badly, so if there was any justification for joining this Coalition to invade Iraq it was Anglo-American relations, the decision to pull out from Anglo-American relations, undoubtedly. Secondly, the reason we are staying, just to repeat it, I think that the British are acting as some form of brake on increased violence in the south.

Q55 Mr Holloway: Do the others agree with that?

Dr Herring: Fundamentally, no; only at the margin, only at the margin. One of the reasons for thinking that is, in terms of the pattern of the violence, there were a number of waves of violence that struck through, the anti-Ba'thist, the anti-Christian, the religious moralist violence, all of which has mostly swept through the Province. Then there is the intra-faction fighting, the mafia fighting, and this keeps sweeping through, and we happen to get caught up in it. If you remember the fiasco in 2004 when the first real military challenge, of course, to the British Forces resulted in the Government headquarters being overrun, the Americans having to come to the rescue; in terms of any real fighting, they were simply incapable. I think my assessment would be it is at the margin and sometimes it is making it worse; so, therefore, do not be there.

Q56 Chairman: What about the important role of training the Armed Forces there?

Dr Rangwala: Could I make just a prior point, because I had a point which followed on from that. There already has been the release of security responsibilities from Muthanna, Maysan and Dhi Qar Provinces by the British, Provinces which the British had a security role in, quite extensively, before 2006. There has been no explosion of violence in those territories.

Dr Dodge: There was in Amara. There was an out-and-out fight between Badr and Sadr in Amara after the British left.

Dr Rangwala: No; that was less than actually were killed in 2004 while the British were still there, in scale. There has been a continuing threat of disputes but there has been no marked increase in the violence in any of those governorates since the British left.

Q57 Mr Hamilton: Dr Dodge, you seemed to indicate that we will damage Anglo-American relationships if we pull out; but that completely ignores the fact that Democrats, who have taken a different position from the Government, argued very strongly on a timetable to leave. How do you come to the conclusion that it will damage Anglo-American relationships if the Democrats win the next election?

Dr Dodge: On two bases. One, the British presence sits across American main supply lines from Kuwait straight up; if the British draw down the Americans will have to send troops down to take their places, which, until a Democrat President, if and until a Democratic President takes office, will damage north-south relations. Secondly, and this is my own interpretation, once the next US President takes office, elected on an undoubtedly Iraqi-sceptic platform, they will look at how they will have to pull out. If you look closely at the fine print and the planning for drawing down, are we talking about a complete cut and run, are we talking about scaling back to the Green Zone or a removal to the fringes; and all of that process will depend on supply lines coming up from Kuwait. It is not black and white, cut and run, with the Democrats. My own interpretation is that it will take most of that first term for a US President to try to work out what they do between a corporate swing and a collapsed state and a civil war in Iraq and an increasingly and totally unpopular occupation in America. I think, as that process unfolds, if we are busy packing up and going home, we are going to engender a deal of resentment at the highest levels of the American Government, even as they are themselves struggling to scale down.

Q58 Chairman: Training: is not the role of the British Army in the Basra area absolutely essential to the training of the Armed Forces there?

Dr Herring: I think the fundamental answer to that has to be no, because training is not the issue, loyalty is the issue. All the forces, all divided by the sectarian political parties, the notion that you can professionalise them and they will stop doing this, because suddenly they realise that professional soldiers do not do these naughty things, is not a description of what is happening at pretty much any level in Iraq. The issue is not training. The ones that were given the most training and were deployed elsewhere in Iraq again are fundamentally useless forces, even the ones that are meant to be the best, that have been deployed in the recent surge offensive, and the Americans are saying, "Well, it turns out they've got no bullets, they're short of uniforms, they're short of radios, they're short of trucks, and actually they tend to be kept that way because we are worried about what they will do." The fundamental issue is loyalty, they are riddled with, as we call them, embedded insurgents; we are not going to train that out of them. It is about politics, it is not about training.

Dr Dodge: You would have to make a distinction between the Army and the Police Force, and I think, if you had a representative of the British military here, they would say that they have had quite a deal of success in training the Army, and probably they would not say it but I would be happy to say it, and the training of the Police has been an abject failure. The Police are responsible for a great deal of kidnapping in Baghdad and have been thoroughly penetrated by the militias in the south. I think it is the Tenth Battalion in the south. The British Army said that they sent forces up to Bagdad and have been seen to be comparatively effective. I think, although undoubtedly there are problems in the Army, they are much, much less, and if you look at opinion poll data that we have both been siting, the Army consistently gets a much higher recognition of trust than the Police Force, which, again, not detracting from the problems inside the Army, indicates the Army has more professionalism, they were sent against the Mahdi Army in Diwaniyah, to some degree of success as well. I think, although the Army has problems, it is more coherent, a more nationalist force than the Police themselves.

Professor Zubaida: I have no special knowledge on military matters but it seems to me that, while Toby is correct on the difference between the Army and the Police, whenever your Army has been entrusted with tasks without American support it has done pretty badly, including in Diyala right now. I wonder to what extent this is a question of lack of training, a lack of resources or insufficient numbers, or perhaps weak motivation.

Q59 Linda Gilroy: Or even expectations being too high, that you can actually train people pretty much from scratch within a year; is that really realistic? Are you saying the military have had some success, that you can expect within a year for us just to draw back completely?

Dr Rangwala: Iraq has had a trained Army, of course, for all of its modern history, so there are many trained Iraqis. The question I do not think does come down to training, in that respect, as my colleagues have said.

Q60 Linda Gilroy: Not recently trained to operate under a democracy, of sorts?

Professor Zubaida: Democracy is laughable.

Dr Rangwala: If one wants to talk opinion polls, and a number of my colleagues have cited opinion polls, I think the most revealing answer in a recent opinion poll from March this year to "Who do you think runs Iraq?" was that over half the population said they believed the US Governments still run Iraq. I think, there, at least, the question of who one is

obeying when one takes one's orders becomes the relevant indicator, not the question of "Can I do this if I want to do this?" which is the training question.

Q61 Linda Gilroy: Was that throughout the whole of Iraq, and we are discussing southern Iraq at the moment and the role of the British in training there. As I have understood it, when we were there last year, there was a programme that would take a period of time; there was always the thought that we would be withdrawing. Clearly, we are not going to say precisely when we are going to withdraw because that would be a hostage to fortune, but we are talking as if that had never been, as if there had never been any differences in the southern area at all, and is not, in fact, the essential difficulty linked to what the US position is? The point drawn out in relation to David Hamilton's question, that in fact you are talking about the lines of exit for the US troops, important lines of exit, being through the south?

Dr Rangwala: I think I would disagree slightly with Dr Dodge on that point; the US can protect the roads and the exit route, as it were, without having to take control of Basra city, in keeping the transit route through from Kuwait. My sense is, at least, that the sense that the Iraqis do not own their country, which I think is prevalent, both amongst the Sunnis as well as amongst the Shi'a population of Iraq, not so much amongst the Kurds but amongst the Arab population of Iraq, is a very damaging one. It is why there is, I think, such rampant corruption, why there is tapping of oil pipelines by political parties which otherwise are in charge of the country. They have those resources at their disposal in any case, but they are still profiteering from the use of these resources on the side because they feel that this is, as it were, "a process that we need to exploit rather than a process that we need to manage," so I think that is a very damaging perception.

Q62 Mr Jenkin: Can I just ask a rather provocative question; there was a poll done in March which suggested that still the majority of Iraqis would not bring back Saddam Hussein. Is it the opinion of Iraqis that it was still the right thing, to get rid of Saddam Hussein, in your view?

Dr Herring: Polling on that has gradually declined to a position where overall nationally you have a relatively even split either way, all things considered. Was it the right thing? You can find one recent poll, in March, when there was actually a very narrow favour saying, all things considered, the invasion was wrong. My recollection was that was the first time ever, but there has been a decline. Obviously, when you break that down in sectarian terms you tend to get a much happier view in the north, which of course mostly was the north-east, which mostly was not occupied, and of course, pretty relentlessly, critical views in Sunni Arab areas. Of course, no-one has asked two million Iraqis, who are now scattered into surrounding countries, how positive they are about the invasion, we suspect they might be pretty not positive, or dead people, if they could vote on this, what they would say. I think it is looking pretty bad, even on that measure now it is not looking good at all, and in terms of what Iraqis are being asked about what they would prefer, a strong man democracy, and so on, the first preference is democracy, as in choosing to change your leader, the second preference is then some form of Islamic state, and the third preference is a strong man for life, and that does trail still, the distant third.

Q63 Chairman: Two million dead; where do you get that figure from?

Dr Herring: No; sorry, two million refugees, so not dead.

Professor Zubaida: From another long-term perspective, and I have seen many years of Iraqi history, every regime change, in its wake, makes people nostalgic for the previous one. I think, given the dire situation in Iraq at the moment, all the previous regimes appear preferable to the present situation.

Mr Hamilton: That is also true of governments.

Chairman: Thank you, gentlemen. Thank you very much indeed for giving up your morning to us in so informative and helpful a way. We are deeply grateful. It was most interesting and helpful. I am now going to declare a short break while we wait for our next witness, but thank you very much indeed.

Witness: **Mr Nadhim Zahawi**, Joint CEO, YouGov, gave evidence.

Q64 Chairman: I am grateful to you for rushing. Please could you introduce yourself and say what the polling that you have given us is based on?

Mr Zahawi: My name is Nadhim Zahawi. I am a Chief Executive of YouGov plc. I also happen to be the son of immigrants to this country; my father is Kurdish, from northern Iraq, and my mother is from Basra. I travel to Iraq quite often. I was there till Friday, for three days, in Urbil. We conduct research across the whole country for the media and for corporates and Government.

Q65 Chairman: Have things in Iraq got better or worse over the last few months, would you say?

Mr Zahawi: In certain governorates and regions the data coming back is things are getting much better, so the picture is obviously uneven.

Q66 Chairman: Which areas are getting better?

Mr Zahawi: Obviously, the north, for example, in the Kurdish region, things are demonstrably better, people have more regular electricity supply, clean water, there is a rebuilding programme taking place, both in the cities and the villages, and so life is much, much better. In most of the southern governorates, people would say life is much, much better for them, too. It is really Baghdad and the Sunni triangle where life is perceived by people as getting much worse since 2003.

Q67 Chairman: That is since 2003, but in recent months, in the last six months, are things getting better or worse?

Mr Zahawi: I would say, incrementally better, but it is within the margin of error.

Q68 Mr Jenkin: Are Coalition Forces still a stabilising element in Iraq, in your view?

Mr Zahawi: Yes, they are, on many levels. One of the great problems is that, obviously, there is no effective Government in Iraq, there are centres of power. The Iraqi Army, in essence, if it were not for the Coalition's influence, would probably break up into those factions; i.e., the Iraqi Army has not coalesced around a Government, a flag, the country, bits of the Iraqi Army have different loyalties.

Q69 Mr Jenkin: We have been hearing how the Iraqi Army is comprised of a rather fluid element, that people collect their weapons and then disappear. Is the Iraqi Army taken of becoming a prevalent force?

Mr Zahawi: My instinct would be, I do not think so. I think that the problem we face is that these power centres call the shots, so you get the Sunni conscripts who will collect their weapons and then go off to Mosul and pass on the weapons to the militias there. The same happens with the Shi'a conscripts, who just go down to whomever they belong to, religiously or politically, it is usually the same thing, in the south of Iraq, and the weapons are just passed on. The problem that you have is that the Government is just not effective, in the sense of bringing everything together. Even the ministries, the way the ministries operate, what you get is, "Oh, well, this ministry belongs to this particular party and therefore we can't do anything with them, because we happen to be from a different party." You really have not got a real Government, you have got these power centres, who have carved up bits of Government for themselves. It is almost a false creation which, without the Coalition being around, would break up into its constituent parts.

Q70 Linda Gilroy: Can the Government develop a capacity and the will to tackle the sort of violence that we have been hearing about this morning? If so, over what timescale?

Mr Zahawi: From what I have witnessed, it can, if you reorganise the Government into what I think is the only solution that is left now, after what has happened over the past three years, and that is into a sort of federation, where you have very clear leaderships in those three different parts of Iraq; there is no other way. If you look at what is happening in the Kurdish region, and already they have had a couple of bombings recently, the leadership there has coalesced around a parliament and a system which now is in control, it has respect for the people, it runs things; of course, there are hurdles still to overcome, but essentially it is in control of that society, the rule of law is respected, in the region. I do not think it is any longer possible to have that as a collective; you almost need to recognise that and break it down into a federation.

The bigger issue is obviously Baghdad, and Baghdad will need to have its own administration; you could have the federation where the president is a rotative president, every year, from the three bits of the country. There is no way a government for the whole is going to carry the country with it. You will have the south saying, "Well, if we're going to have a Sunni in control we're just not going to join in;" the Sunnis saying, "Well, a Shi'a is in control; of course, he's not going to do us any favours," and whatever. You need to, I think, really look at the structure of government in Iraq and simply just accept the fact that actually it is made up of three different countries.

Q71 Linda Gilroy: I take it that you feel that the Iraqi Government has been totally unsuccessful at bridging the sectarian divide?
Mr Zahawi: Absolutely. On the face of it, they will all sit round a single table and appear to be a government, but the reality on the ground, you do not have to go very far into any ministry to realise that basically it is power bases, it is completely factional.

Q72 Chairman: What is your perception of the way the US surge has gone down, with the presence of more American troops?
Mr Zahawi: The data coming back from Baghdad is, and we run a tracking study in Baghdad which looks at how people perceive security in the capital, it is getting better, but people think it has just simply been displaced, rather than it has actually gone away completely. Part of the problem is you have got this feeling that "Actually they are not going to have the stomach to be here for very long and therefore why should I put my head over the parapet and start co-operating, because if they're not going to be around these militias are going to come back, and therefore basically I'd better align myself with whoever has got the biggest gun to protect me."

Q73 Chairman: What about British troops; what would be the reaction to the withdrawal of British troops?
Mr Zahawi: I think that, obviously, what you have in the south, where the British presence is, is a situation where at least one of the factions there would like rid of us as soon as possible, because they need to exert more control over the region, heavily backed by Iran in that area. I think that the people would feel much less secure if we left, so the silent majority would feel it a betrayal, because there would be huge amounts of blood shed and factional infighting to take control of the area, between SCIRI and the Mahdi Army or the Da'wa.

Q74 Mr Hamilton: We have just heard from previous witnesses, a number of them, that the British have a hands-off attitude in the south and therefore they were encouraging the view that if the Brits move out very little will change in the south?
Mr Zahawi: There is a difference between hands-off but being there with a big stick, if necessary, and not being there at all and the factions which were co-operating with the Coalition then becoming exposed to just slaughter, essentially.

Q75 Mr Hamilton: Could I ask, Chairman, with your permission, an answer to a previous question indicated that we should look at a federation rather than the separation of countries: what do you prefer?
Mr Zahawi: I think a federation would be the most preferred route for, I would say, all the groups, including the Kurds. In terms of the Kurds, I think a separation, if you talked to the leaderships there, would be very unhealthy for them, especially the recent troubles with Turkey. Certainly a federation, co-operation over things like having a rolling presidency, co-operation over Baghdad, creating a form of government for Baghdad in which all three can participate, would probably be the most preferable route.

Q76 Mr Holloway: If you saw a federation emerge, would you see large movements of population, as we saw in the Balkans in the early nineties, where minority groups would go to their areas?
Mr Zahawi: Sadly, a lot of it has happened already. Baghdad obviously is an extreme version of that; i.e., that the Sunni population of Baghdad is down to about 11%. People have either moved out to Sunni areas or have left for Syria or Jordan, or the Kurdish region.

Q77 Mr Holloway: So the answer is yes?
Mr Zahawi: Yes; absolutely.

Q78 Mr Holloway: How much more do you see though in the rest of the country, what sorts of numbers would be moving around?
Mr Zahawi: The bit that it will depend on obviously is where you draw the boundaries, so, again, the Kirkuk issue, for example; if that ends up being rolled into the Kurdish federal area then you might see bigger proportions of movement. Really it depends; it is very hard to put your finger on it. Obviously, as you have seen and you have witnessed, there has been an exodus anyway of the Sunni population away from areas which are becoming dominated by the Shi'as in Baghdad.

Q79 Chairman: Mr Zahawi, thank you very much indeed for coming to help us. You have a busy life in YouGov, I know, but it is good to hear that you are doing stuff in Iraq as well as in this country.
Mr Zahawi: Thank you very much and I apologise for keeping you, for the delay. I got my timing wrong.
Chairman: Thank you very much.

Tuesday 24 July 2007

Members present

Mr James Arbuthnot, in the Chair

Mr David S Borrow	Mr Bernard Jenkin
Mr David Crausby	Mr Brian Jenkins
Linda Gilroy	Mr Kevan Jones
Mr Dai Havard	Robert Key
Mr Adam Holloway	Willie Rennie

Witnesses: **Rt Hon Bob Ainsworth MP**, Minister of State for the Armed Forces, **Mr Desmond Bowen CMG**, Policy Director, and **Brigadier Chris Hughes CBE**, Director of Joint Commitments (Military), Ministry of Defence, gave evidence.

Q80 Chairman: Welcome to this evidence session on Iraq and, Minister, without meaning to say anything about your team, may I say you are particularly welcome at your first session before this Committee. We are conscious that you are newly in post, but we are also conscious of the fact that you have just returned from Iraq. We were in Iraq a couple of weeks ago, as you know, and some of the people we met were in the RAF Regiment which has just suffered those casualties in Basra and, I must say, we were deeply impressed with the courage of what the RAF Regiment were doing and of the sorts of trials that they are all going through in Basra at the moment. The casualties have risen and you will have been there last week, although I do not know whether you were there when they were actually killed, but thank you very much indeed for coming in front of our Committee. May I ask you to begin by introducing your team, please.
Mr Ainsworth: Chairman, thank you for your welcome. As you say, I have been in post for less than a month, but I have managed to get out to both Afghanistan and Iraq in the last week. With me, I have Desmond Bowen, who is our Policy Director, and Brigadier Chris Hughes, who is the Military Director of Joint Commitments. Chris not only holds that position, but, prior to that, in 2005 he was Operation Commander out in Basra, so he brings a knowledge probably far deeper than yours or mine. Recognising the fact that I am pretty new into the job, we will try to act as a team in order to try to give you the maximum amount of information that we can. In coming up to speed, I am trying as fast as I can, but I do not want my coming up to speed to hinder your ability to get the information that you need to get out of the Department in order to conduct the inquiry. Your comments about the people out there, I was on my way into the COB at the time that the attack took place, so my arrival was actually delayed by what happened and, as I say, I was just enormously impressed not only with the bravery of the troops there, but the competence, the skill and the ability that is required at every level of the operation by our forces out in Iraq is tremendously impressive.

Q81 Chairman: Can I begin this evidence session by asking what your general assessment is of the security and political situation in Iraq as a whole.

Do you think things have got better or worse and what do you think the prospects are overall for Iraq as a whole? We will come down to the southern part later.
Mr Ainsworth: I did not manage to get up to Baghdad. We laid the trip on at fairly short notice, so that was not possible as people's diary commitments had taken them off, so I would not try to pretend to the Committee that my knowledge and assessment of the overall situation would be as good as it is about the circumstances in the south-east area where we have direct responsibility. We are in the middle of the American operation, the Surge, and that has had success in some areas, but it is far too early to say the degree to which that has been successful and obviously there is the big report coming up in September.

Q82 Chairman: We will come back to the Surge itself in due course and we will ask some more detailed questions.
Mr Ainsworth: I would say that the nature of the problem in different parts of the country is very different, as the Committee will know better than I. We have got the sectarian problems in the Baghdad area in the centre of the country dominating the situation and the need for the Iraqi Government to reach out to the Sunni community is overwhelming in terms of the necessity in that area. In our area of responsibility, the nature of the problem is completely different where religion is not part of the problem, potentially it is a force for unity in our own area, but we are dealing with a different set of problems and a different set of priorities in the south-east.

Q83 Chairman: If we can move on to the south-eastern area, how would you assess the security and political situation in the south-eastern area, particularly in the Basra province?
Mr Ainsworth: I think the recent appointment of General Mohan to command the Armed Forces in the south-east and General Jalil to command the police forces in the area is very important and a good sign of potential. Those people, having been appointed, now need to be backed up. Progress with regards to army capability and army capacity is a lot more reassuring than it is in the area of the police. The police have got a lot more work to do as the

problems are far deeper and more difficult to deal with, but Mohan has made a very good start, as has General Jalil. The capacity of the Iraqi 10th Division is coming along, it is being built all the time, and it will be absolutely vital that that continues if we are going to be able to achieve provincial Iraqi control in Basra, as we have in the other three areas. Meanwhile, the position that we find ourselves in is difficult, as the Committee knows. We are the people who are effectively providing the backbone of stability and, therefore, those people in the area, no matter what their motivations are, and there are so many different motivations of different people in the Basra region through to people who have very close associations with forces outside the country, there are the patriotic kind of youth who are targeting our forces, but there is also a huge, criminal element who are effectively intent on pillaging their own country, people should not underestimate the degree to which that motivates some of the forces in the south-east area. Those people know that we are the ultimate guarantor of any chance of progress and, therefore, it is not surprising, although it is enormously difficult, that we are the people who are being targeted overwhelmingly by those individuals concerned. That puts us in some difficulty. Convoys into the Basra Palace are very difficult to secure and the attacks on Basra Palace are regular, as are attacks out on to the COB itself. Our presence there though not only is a necessity in terms of the capacity-building, the training that is going on in the area, but it also is our ability to project force into the wider province which, until the assessment is done that the Iraqi security services are able to take over, is a necessity which will remain.

Q84 Chairman: You used one phrase which I wonder if you could explain, please. You said "patriotic youth". Are there Iraqi patriots there attacking our forces, were you suggesting?
Mr Ainsworth: I think that there are young people in the Basra area who are being used. Their motivation is not necessarily the motivation of those people who are putting them on the streets and who are using them in order to attack. There are serious organised militias who have, as I have said, different motivations and some of them are closely aligned with forces in Iran and some of them have a clear, nationalist commitment to Iraq itself, but nonetheless, want to attack us and some of them are looking after their corrupt individual self-interest, and I do not think we should downplay that, but not everybody is of that mind. There are lots of innocent people who are being used by those organisations who have not necessarily got that motivation at all.

Q85 Mr Jones: Can I just pick up a couple of points you have made. You used the words "ultimate guarantor", "projector of force" and "we are the backbone of stability". When we visited a few weeks ago, it was my fifth visit to Iraq and my fifth visit to Basra and my first visit was in July 2003 when we quite clearly had a footprint in the city of Basra where we had people on the ground, you could walk around, you had civic teams doing reconstruction

and things like that. Is it not the case that what we have now basically is a force surrounded, I think, a little bit like cowboys and Indians, at Basra Palace with the reinforcements, you could say, at the COB at the airport? The idea that we are projecting force or stability is just not the case. We are going in on basically nightly suicide missions on occasions to go in to relieve the palace and, once we withdraw from the palace, the city itself, there will be very little need for us to go in and, if we did, it would be extremely dangerous, so are we actually a stability force or a projector of power anymore or are we actually just really leading Basra itself to what it is, controlled by various factions, as you have described?
Mr Ainsworth: As we get nearer the point where people begin to appreciate that there is the prospect of the Government of Iraq having the ability to control the situation itself, then those people who do not want that to happen—

Q86 Mr Jones: No, but we are not doing it like that.
Mr Ainsworth: Those people who have a vested interest in ensuring that it cannot happen obviously become pretty focused on what they have to do in order to try to prevent that from coming about.
Mr Jones: But we are not doing that. What we are doing basically, there are two or three lines or routes into Basra Palace and we were told quite clearly by the people who were going in that night when we were there a few weeks ago—
Mr Jenkin: That is confidential.

Q87 Mr Jones: Shut up, Bernard, stop being prissy! Those lines or routes into the town were being attacked not occasionally, but on a nightly basis going in.
Mr Ainsworth: We have to get convoys into the palace and there are not that many routes by which those convoys, and they are supply convoys, as you know, because you have been out there more often than I have, so you have probably got a far better understanding of this than me, but those convoys are substantial and there are only a very few routes that can be taken in there, so that is a massive operation to try to provide force protection and to keep people alive while we manage to reinforce the palace. Now, I am not trying to say that that is not a difficult issue, but it is not true to say that our presence either in the palace or in the COB does not provide the last guarantee of power in the region and the 10th Division is not ready, although it may be approaching that point, to assume those responsibilities itself. Now, we are getting there and the capacity of the 10th Division is coming up all the time, they are training 5th Brigade now, they are beginning to be brought up to strength now, but, for the time being, the ultimate guarantor or the biggest boys on the block effectively are us and our presence there is felt and it is felt where we need it to be felt. We are able, although it is very difficult, to take forces into the city itself and that happens on a regular basis, and we are able to deploy out into the areas around the city, so it is not true to say that our presence there is not a projective force in the area to a considerable degree.

Mr Jones: Well, I would disagree with you on that.

Chairman: I will come back to these issues because they are very important.

Q88 Robert Key: Minister, I would like to take a step back and look at the politics of this because a lot of people in this country are now asking, "Why are we still there and what are we trying to achieve?" The Iraq Commission, in their recent report, concluded, "The initial, over-ambitious vision of the Coalition can no longer be achieved in Iraq", and, "The UK Government needs . . . to redefine its objectives". How do you respond to that?

Mr Ainsworth: Well, for some long time now we have concentrated on the need for security and stability and those have been a large part of our objectives. When you say, "Why are we still there?", we are there in lower numbers than we were some short while ago and we have managed to hand over control of three of the four provinces that we originally had direct responsibility for to the Iraqi forces themselves. Basra is more difficult and it is more difficult than those three provinces; there is no doubt about that. We are there in order to achieve the conditions where they are able to take over the job that we are currently doing. Now, there is hope among our people out there at every level that we are approaching the situation where that can be done, but we have got to look at the conditions that apply on the ground, their capacity, and we have got to talk to our allies and to the Iraqi Government about that. That cannot be a unilateral decision on our part; it has got to be a proper assessment of the conditions and the capability of the people we are handing over to as well.

Q89 Robert Key: How do we make that assessment then? How do we measure our success?

Mr Ainsworth: It has to be to a degree subjective, but it has to be done in consultation with Iraqi commanders and there is growing confidence on their part. I even met General Habib who appears to be a fairly competent commander of 10th Division and he is getting to the point where certainly he thinks that his forces are able to take over in Basra city in the near future, and that is where he is, so that conversation is ongoing. Are we able to hand over in the city, are they up to taking over not only the facilities that we have got, but doing the job that we are doing as well and then are they able to take over in the wider Basra province? That conversation is taking place.

Q90 Robert Key: The Iraq Commission said that the "handover should not be dependent on the prevailing security situation". Do you agree with that?

Mr Ainsworth: No, I do not think I do agree with that. I think that the security position cannot be the whole picture, but it is a vital part of the assessment of whether or not we are able to hand over. We cannot hand over to a vacuum or to the forces that are going to destroy Iraqi Government control and want to destroy Iraqi Government control in the south-east of the country and, if we do not want to do that, then security is absolutely key and the capacity of the people we are handing over to is absolutely key to the timetable for handing over control of the province.

Q91 Robert Key: So we will not be driven out by a difficult security situation, but our objective will be to leave in an orderly manner when the Iraqi forces can look after themselves and their Government and people? Is that a fair assessment?

Mr Ainsworth: Build the capacity, assess the situation and check the confidence of the people we are handing over to, and that is not to say that there are not going to be problems the other side of the handover; there are problems now. Iraq is not a benign environment, and those provinces that we have handed over have not been trouble-free and there have been problems in those provinces, but the important point is that, when those problems occurred, the Iraqis dealt with it themselves. They dealt with it themselves, they controlled the situation and they coped with the problems. Now, that has got to be what we have got to try and achieve in Basra.

Q92 Mr Jones: Can I return to the military and ask quite a simple question to start off with and a few follow-ups. What is the current military role for UK Forces in Basra?

Mr Ainsworth: I think we have talked about it already, although you disagree with me about what the effect of that is. The role is to liaise, to train and to build capacity in the Iraqi Forces themselves and to exercise some projection of force out into the wider area in order to allow that capacity to develop. I do believe that, if we hand over prematurely, then that will be a major problem. Now, that is not to say that we might not be approaching the point when we are able to do that, and there are lots of people out there who hope we are getting close to the point where the Iraqis would be able to take responsibility for the province and, as I say, those conversations, those discussions are taking place.

Q93 Mr Jones: One of the things that we were told by numerous people in the military while we were there is that 90% of the actual violence and attacks are actually against Coalition Forces. Now, it chimes obviously with General Dannatt's position, and I will come on to him in a minute, but this is a quote from *The Daily Telegraph* which seems to be the way that he now influences public policy by leaking things to *The Daily Telegraph* rather than talking to ministers or this Committee and it says, "The plain-speaking officer . . . suggested that the British presence in Iraq was 'exacerbating the security problems' and warned that the Army would 'break' if it was kept there too long". What is your reaction to that?

Mr Ainsworth: If you are intent on mayhem and chaos, no matter what your motives are, whether they are political or whether they are corrupt self-interest—

Q94 Mr Jones: We are talking about General Dannatt now, are we!

Mr Ainsworth: I am talking about those individuals who are attacking our forces all the time. Then yes, it is right to a degree, and nobody denies this, that it is a useful tool to be able to focus on the fact that there are foreign forces in the area in order to be able to mobilise people who would not necessarily share your aims and objectives, so it is not surprising that people can be motivated to attack us, but those are the motivations.

Mr Jones: But the concern which I have and I think some others on this Committee have is that when you have a senior general, like General Dannatt, making statements like that, and it annoys me intensely because, whenever we have any senior military general before this Committee and we ask about overstretch, we are told that everything is all right and it is no problem, but it does concern me as to who is actually in control now. If we have a general who is leaking stuff to the newspapers left, right and centre, trying clearly to influence whatever agenda it is, is there a big fissure opening up between the politicians and the MoD and General Dannatt because, if that is the case, then I think that is very serious?

Chairman: It is not established that it is General Dannatt who leaked it and you may wish to comment on that as well.

Q95 Mr Jones: It is very strange mail they seem to get regularly at *The Daily Telegraph*.

Mr Ainsworth: I do not think it is any secret, with the amount of people that we have deployed in Iraq and Afghanistan, that there are not huge reserves around for contingencies and other things that might apply, and that is basically the information that was put into the public domain. There is not anything new in it. Now, we cannot control how the media choose to report on something that has been known for some long time. We have got two battle groups that are deployable effectively in unforeseen circumstances at the moment and no more than that because of the amount of commitment that we have got in these two ongoing, as termed within the Department, "medium-sized commitments", and that is a very large commitment. Now, the reporting of defence matters often gets tweaked and gets taken in all kinds of different directions. There were internal documents that basically said what everybody has known for some time that were, it seems, leaked to a newspaper and they chose to put it on the front page, but when I read it, I was wondering where the news was, where the actual news was in the story.

Q96 Mr Jones: Actually, I have to say, I sympathise with General Dannatt's position, although I disagree possibly with his methods of actually trying to change the policy direction, but it was put to us in Iraq and, I have to say, it is something I am actually now coming to myself, that the real military objectives for us in Basra have actually finished and that actually the process which is going to ultimately bring security there is going to be a political one and the fact that the only reason why we are actually not withdrawing more quickly is because relations with the United States are actually influencing that. Now,

that, I think, is going to create problems not just politically, but I think also militarily because quite clearly, talking to people on the ground and the dedication which the Chairman and you have already alluded to, if the military reason for them being there is no longer there, you can understand them getting pretty cheesed off pretty quickly. The concern I have is that, if we are going to just pull back to the COB and sit there, we are going to get unfortunately more tragedies like we had last weekend. Now, is that a price worth paying for keeping US-UK relations on some type of civilised basis or for saving face?

Mr Ainsworth: We are part of a coalition in Iraq and we were voluntarily part of the Coalition in Iraq and consulting with our allies about what we do, when we do it and how we do it is an important part of being part of the Coalition, indeed it is absolutely essential to being part of the Coalition and, if there are people who are suggesting that we ought not to do that, then the ramifications of that are pretty profound, but what you are saying about Basra is true. It is the politics and the economics that are important, but our presence there has until now been needed in order to make those things happen. Now, the very fact that we have been able to point up to the Iraqis that we are serious about handing over to them and the fact that we have handed over to them in three of those four provinces has concentrated the mind. The appointment of General Mohan and the appointment of General Jalil is a response from the Iraqis, I think, to the recognition that their getting a grip of their security arrangements in Basra is increasingly important and that we are not prepared to hold on for ever while they get to a position some time whenever, so there is a concentration of the mind, yes, but the advance that needs to be made is in the political and the economic area.

Q97 Mr Jones: But the fact that Mohan is not actually getting control of the security situation and is actually doing deals with the actual militia in the city, and I am not criticising him for that, that is a political thing rather than a security or military solution to it?

Mr Ainsworth: Well, in any insurgency situation, you try to do an assessment of who the enemy is, what their motivation is, who is winnable and who is irreconcilable and, if you have any sense, you try to split them up and you do not leave them as a consolidated front against you. If General Mohan is doing that, then all strength to his elbow; that is the job that we want him to do.

Q98 Willie Rennie: I have a slightly different view from yourself of when we visited Iraq. I came away with the firm belief that, with 90% of the attacks on our forces and, if we withdrew, then the violence which would result would be self-limiting over a relatively short period, we are now part of the problem and not part of the solution. Now, whichever way you look at it, whether you believe that our effort in the south has been a success or whether you think it has been a failure, I think you would come to the same conclusion that our broader withdrawal is something that is quite urgent and would actually resolve for the longer term some of the problems in the south because, as you have recognised, the south is quite different from other parts of the country. Finally, when we met the Prime Minister, we asked him the question, "What would be the effect of our withdrawal from the south?", and I am summarising here, but he said that they could cope with the withdrawal.

Mr Ainsworth: I agree with what you are saying, that the violence in the south appears to be self-limiting. We do not see the suicide bombers and we do not see the degree of irreconcilability to the institutions themselves of the Iraqi State that we do in some other parts of the country. There are other influences in Basra that are not conducive to nation-building, but a lot of the people, and some of them are attacking us, their fundamental aim is to make Iraq a successful country and, therefore, there is potential there that is not in other parts of the area. As to how quickly we can get out, I can only say what I have already said and that is that it has got to be based on the conditions and it has got to be based on the capability of the people we are taking over from, but that debate is taking place now.

Q99 Mr Havard: This question about the self-limiting violence should we withdraw and so on, it is more nationalistic in the south and it is nihilistic in the middle, as one way of describing it, around Baghdad and, therefore, these political possibilities are there, but the question I want to go back to is about this statement attributed to General Dannatt, and I do not know whether he has leaked anything to anybody, but it is in the paper and I want to know what the effects are because, it seems to me, there is a series of phases. As you rightly say, if we withdraw from the town, we are back in the base, but that is not the end of the story and there are a number of other phases that have to go in the story and the same with the US, but let us be clear. The quote that was given before, he is said to have said that our presence in Iraq "was exacerbating the security problems" and he warned that the Army would "break" if we were there too long. Now, that is not the Iraqi Army, that is the British Army which would break if we were there too long, so the question of timing of all of these developments is crucial. Now, he is also reported as saying that he wants extra infantry units. Now, if Iraq is, and it rightly is, stimulating a whole discussion about our formation of forces and how many commitments we can take on, et cetera, et cetera, can we actually have a proper, structured discussion about that rather than it coming out in the newspaper on the basis that it is currently doing because I think, from talking to the personnel on the ground there, that they know that? They know that their military utility is running out and they say, "We are the wrong tool for the job. We do not contest that the job needs to be done, but we are not the best people to do it", so, if it is not them, who is it and how do we have that debate?

Mr Ainsworth: The 'who is it' is the Iraqis themselves. Everybody recognises that.

Q100 Mr Havard: But we are talking about the British Army "breaking" if we do not do something here. That is what the general said and that is what I want to contest. I think some of this is hyperbole in all of this, but nevertheless, we need to have a proper assessment. That is what being said by the top military commander, that our Army is about to "break", and that has elevated this discussion to a slightly different level.

Mr Ainsworth: There are a number of things that you have said. The 'who is it' is the Iraqis, as we have all acknowledged and I not think we disagree with. If we get out of Basra Palace and get back to the COB, then the nature of the problem that we will face will change. Now, whether or not it will get worse is a matter of opinion. There are things, and I will ask the Brigadier to come in in a minute and fill out what his views are on that, but some of the things we currently have to do we will no longer have to do, like the convoys into the palace, so there will be less of a job and less danger in that regard. Some of the weaponry that is being used against the palace is not usable against the COB because of sheer distances and you cannot lob short range mortars into the COB without coming out of a built-up area and these people use their own people as shelters, so they do their dirty business from among the populated areas, but there is no doubt that some of the capacity that is currently being used against the palace will potentially be usable against the COB.

Q101 Mr Havard: But then we have got 5,000 personnel in the COB, stuck there, doing what for how long?

Mr Ainsworth: On this issue that you raise about whether or not the Army will "break", and you have been out to Iraq recently yourself, I was out last week and nobody in theatre said that to me.

Q102 Mr Havard: No, exactly—

Mr Ainsworth: They are enormously—

Q103 Mr Havard:—but they did to *The Daily Telegraph.*

Mr Ainsworth: They are enormously taxed about the way ahead, they are enormously taxed about improving force protection, but nobody has used those kinds of words to me and I do not believe they used them to you either. I do not know whether the Brigadier wants to say anything in terms of these issues of how we protect ourselves in the COB, if we get out of Basra Palace.

Brigadier Hughes: If I may pick up on a couple of points, I think the discussion well illustrates that we are at the most difficult time, that any military transition, as transition is in other wars, is hugely complex and it has been getting more difficult as we get closer to transition. Does that mean we are part of the problem and not part of the solution? I do not think so, not for the people who matter, that is to say, the Government of Iraq.

Q104 Mr Havard: That is not what General Dannatt says.

Brigadier Hughes: We are part of the problem as far as quite a lot of Shia militant fighters are concerned in south-east Iraq, in Basra. We are absolutely part of the solution as far as the Government of Iraq is concerned. If we are to make sure in the very difficult, dangerous fight for wealth and power that is going on in Basra that the Government of Iraq is actually going to have to have a say, then we still play a significant part in backing that up as guarantors, as the Minister said. As to the issue of whether, when we come out of Basra Palace, things are going to get much worse in the COB and the fact that 85/90% of the attacks are against us and, therefore, if we were not there, would not be happening, it is hugely difficult to ascertain that. People have got it wrong on a number of occasions in the last couple of years by trying to forecast where we are going to be within a set time limit, in six months or 12 months, which is why we have consistently given this message about it being condition-based. We have an idea of what we think will happen when Basra Palace is handed back. We have an idea of what we think, and plans for what we think, will happen when we get provincial Iraqi control in Basra, but we cannot be certain about that because there are so many shifting dynamics that we need to be alive to the fact that we keep with the conditions and, when the conditions allow, we are then able to make another move, and that is why it has been so difficult, nay impossible, to put a time-frame on it.

Q105 Mr Jenkin: Would you describe victory in this rather unsatisfactory situation as the handing over of security and political control in Basra province to forces which are answerable to the Iraqi Government which can control the situation in Basra, if not necessarily create Hampstead Garden Suburb, and the orderly withdrawal of the British and Coalition Forces from southern Iraq? Would that constitute victory in the circumstances?
Brigadier Hughes: I think it has been quite a long time since anybody has talked about victory in Iraq and I certainly would not try and define victory in Iraq; I think it is the wrong word. I think we can try and define success and that is in line with the strategy that we are following at the moment. It is about making sure that the people, through the national Government and the provincial Government, have a say about how they run their lives in Basra and elsewhere and can, through that share of the national and provincial governments, lead a reasonable life. It is about making sure that the criminal elements that the Minister has talked about, the militant on militant and the various political parties down there do not grab the cake and cut it amongst themselves and leave out the Government and the people of Basra, and it is about us coming away in good order. Those are the sorts of definitions that we would see laid out for success rather than victory, Mr Jenkin.

Q106 Mr Jenkin: So we can safely assume that success is achievable, otherwise you would not be sitting here and that would not be the military advice that the Minister would be accepting, and we can safely assume that we believe that to be achievable?
Mr Ainsworth: Success is achievable in those terms.

Q107 Mr Jenkin: In those very limited terms.
Mr Ainsworth: Hampstead Garden Suburb, as you said, it will be a long, long time before we get to that.

Q108 Mr Jenkin: Therefore, a timetable for precipitate withdrawal would threaten that success?
Mr Ainsworth: Yes.

Q109 Mr Jenkin: And we need to understand that?
Mr Ainsworth: Yes.
Mr Jones: Can I just come back, Brigadier, to what you have just said and just reiterate what General Dannatt said, that we are "exacerbating the security problems" and he warned that the Army would "break" if we kept it there too long. Now, I have to say, it is a position I sympathise with and, although I perhaps do not approve of his methods of getting a message across through the newspapers, this is clearly a big division between the official line that is coming out of the MoD that somehow we are not the problem and, I have to say, when we were in Iraq, it is a position which is actually shared by some senior people on the ground in Basra, that we are becoming the problem. If you have got a senior military figure saying that, if we stay there too long, the Army is going to "break", that is a very serious position. Now, you are saying that we are not part of the problem, so clearly there is a division there, but someone is either wrong or there is this huge division between the MoD and General Dannatt. Now, both cannot be right and, if we have got that huge chasm which is clearly there and, I have to say, I do concur more with General Dannatt's position on this than I do the MoD's position, but someone has got to get some reality into this because, if we do not, we are going to have a situation whereby not only are we going to continue being the problem, but we are actually going to lose more people there and, if the general is right, it is going to have tremendous effects on the ability of, and morale in, the Army. Therefore, someone has got to be honest and say that General Dannatt is right or actually sack him.

Q110 Chairman: It may be better for the Minister to answer that question.
Mr Ainsworth: We are not planning to keep the levels of force in south-east Iraq that we have got currently there over the long term. We are actively in the process of handing over to the Iraqis. We have handed over three provinces and we are now in discussions on the fourth province. We are going to be able to take down numbers to some degree if we achieve that fourth province handover and we go to over-watch in the fourth province, but we are still going to have to, for a period of time, and I am not prepared to define the period of time, keep sufficient people there to be able to provide that ultimate back-up and to protect themselves, but we are not

planning to stay in the numbers that we are currently in south-east Iraq over the long period. What the Committee thinks General Dannatt has done or has not done, and I am not dead sure we are not conflating two stories here, and there have been recently some comments that were attributed to him from, how long ago, a year ago or something like that and maybe the Committee needs to talk to General Dannatt about it—

Mr Jones: Minister, let us be clear. What I would say to you is they may think, "We may need just to keep it going for a bit longer then and the Brits are going to break and they will off", and this does not play very well actually in that theatre when you are trying to do a job. Frankly, this is the sort of thing that plays into the hands of the opposition rather than helping you do a constructive job on the ground. That is my concern.

Q111 Chairman: Minister, your own reaction to this memorandum was that you said that it was the sort of information that had been around for years and you were yourself surprised that it was front-page news.

Mr Ainsworth: I think I saw the story while I was out there. I am not dead certain about that, but I think I saw the story while I was out there. I could not understand, I think it was, was it, the front page of *The Telegraph* that I saw, and I did not know why it was on the front page of *The Telegraph*. I have seen papers over the period since I have been appointed and that says that there is not an awful lot left in the locker, that we have got a couple of battle groups with the commitments that we have got at the moment to respond to circumstances that may arise, so why someone would take that comment from a leaked document and stick it on the front page of a national newspaper, that was my reaction to it, that I did not quite understand it.

Mr Holloway: I would like to ask Mr Bowen what sort of numbers do you think we might be in in Iraq in five years' time and what sort of conjecture have you done with regard to American force levels, say, in five years' time with, as we know, a change in president, and is it true that they are building bases for the very long term?

Chairman: I would like to stop that question there because we are just about to get on to a slightly different question that moves in the same general direction from David Crausby, but Brian Jenkins, you wanted to fill in.

Mr Jenkins: Yes, Chairman, a few minutes ago, on the same issue.

Chairman: There was a queue.

Q112 Mr Jenkins: I know, there is always a queue. Minister, you will be aware of the situation in Basra. When you refer to criminality and small, petty criminality at times, Sunni militia are not small or petty criminals, and they may be a part of the solution as well as being a part of the problem. Have you considered and looked at what approach we can take in establishing the rule of law—which we are all obliged to do—in Basra, when you know these militias are funded by the large-scale theft of oil.

You know that the measuring equipment has been switched off so that no one can tell how much oil they have been pinching, you know that this stuff goes into a port, it is brought on board a tanker and the tanker sails out. This is not something that can slip out in the middle of the night, so who is responsible for trying to control the export of this stolen oil and the funding of the militia? Is it somebody maybe in the Government that is overseeing this operation, because this militia is a long term ally of theirs; how do we come to grips with this? Our Forces are not the right people to do this possibly, but what is the situation with regard to the large scale theft of this oil which is funding the struggle against us?

Mr Ainsworth: I hope I did not refer to petty criminality; I am sure there is petty criminality going on in Basra as there is in my own constituency, Coventry North East. It is the grand scale criminality that is a huge part of the problem in the south, there is no doubt about it; we are not dealing with the sectarian divide as they are in other parts of Iraq, these people are religiously and ethnically cohesive, but there are sections of the community there and the power structures there who are lining their own pockets at the expense of their own people. The whole purpose of our supporting the Iraqi security forces in terms of the police and the army and urging the Government to take effective action and trying to advise them on the action that they are taking, in order to try to get a grip of that the Iraqi Government need to appreciate the huge importance of Basra. It is their window on the world, 85% to 90% of their wealth goes out through that city, it is of vital importance to the future of Iraq. The very fact that we have started the process of handing control to the Iraqi security forces has focused the mind on the dangers from their point of view. I do not think that we would have seen the appointments of Mohan and Jalil, with the kind of remit that I hope they have been given to do, if that focus had not come to the fore. We can only hope that those appointments continue to achieve the good start that they have made and that they are backed up when they start to take the difficult decisions that they are going to have to take. The police in particular; if we are going to be able to sort out some of the problems that there are with the police, where corruption and infiltration has been a difficulty, then there are going to have to be difficult things done by the command structure and the Government of Iraq is going to have to back them up. We are going to have to inform the Government of Iraq and support the Government of Iraq in those difficult decisions they have to take over the coming period.

Q113 Mr Jenkins: But these are tankers, Ministers. These are actually tankers that are sailing out with stolen oil. If we are in control of the Straits, if we are in control of the port, how can they slip past us? Who is turning a blind eye here?

Mr Ainsworth: There is no turning of a blind eye on the part of British Forces; British Forces gather intelligence, try to exercise what force and power that they can and are trying to build the capacity of the Iraqis themselves so that we have an Iraqi solution to an Iraqi problem. As the Brigadier said earlier, the people who want us out are the people who have a vested interest in that continuing; it is not the Government of Iraq, it is the people who have a vested interest in that continuing and them being allowed to continue to rip off their own people; they are the people who want us out.

Q114 Chairman: Minister, before we move on can I ask one question arising out of something you said, namely that one of the important roles of the British military is to train the Iraqi Army. A witness who came before us a month ago said that the issue is not training, it is loyalty. How would you comment on that?
Mr Ainsworth: The issue is training, there is a capacity problem. We have almost single-handedly taken on the role of trying to recreate the Iraqi Navy down at Um-Qasr, actually giving them the ability to do the job. That is an important part of it and we should not just wipe that off the board, but loyalty is hugely important. Certainly, the commanders of the Army need to know that the Army is on side for what they are attempting to achieve, and that is stability, loyalty to an Iraqi state. That has got to be the first priority; Mohan and Habib recognise that and they recognise the importance of that and, yes, I would put that higher than training.

Q115 Chairman: But if you would put loyalty higher than training you would accept, I think, that loyalty cannot be imposed by foreign troops.
Mr Ainsworth: No, it cannot be imposed by foreign troops.
Brigadier Hughes: There is clearly an issue of loyalty and affiliation, whether that be tribal or familial or political. What we have found with the Iraqi Army is that working outside their own area, outside their own locale, they have been impressive on a number of operations, not least the three battalions of the 10th Division who have been working in Baghdad as part of the current surge operation. Where we have had difficulties is where Basra battalions or those recruited from Basra have been asked to work in Basra, and you can imagine the reasons why, it must be immensely difficult for them. That is why, as part of the plan to bring an additional brigade, as part of a new division, into South East Iraq, one of the plans that General Habib is looking at, the commander of 10 Div, is to switch the battalions around so that those from Basra will work in Dhi Qar and those from Dhi Qar will work in Basra in order to try and get away from those local serious difficulties and challenges that the loyalty issue makes them face, Chairman.
Chairman: That is very helpful, thank you. David Crausby.

Q116 Mr Crausby: You made the comment, Minister, that we are not planning to stay in Iraq long term.

Mr Ainsworth: In the numbers we are at the moment.

Q117 Mr Crausby: And that was very much supported last week when the Ministry of Defence announced a further reduction in troops of 500 conditional upon the handover of Basra Palace to Iraqi security control. Can you tell us something about the process of drawdown and what conditions will be necessary for us to make some further progress. I understand the legitimate sensitivity about numbers and I accept that you would not want to give us that kind of detail, but can you give us some indication as to what the conditions would be?
Mr Ainsworth: You would like to lure me there in any case. On the kind of timescales that were mentioned before it is enormously difficult to think in those timescales, based on what we have got at the moment. We have got a plan that we are working on to get out of the city and to hand over the facilities that we have got in the city. We have managed successfully to hand over other facilities; the Iraqis have gone in and occupied and taken control. The next stage to that is provincial Iraqi control and we think that we can achieve that in the near future. To try to see what the consequences of that are is enormously difficult. What will be the reaction of these various forces that are currently fighting over the spoils in Basra city; if we are not there and they are not able to focus on us, does that give a new opportunity to people like General Mohan to peel off certain elements of them to gain the loyalty of parts of them to get effective control? It is very difficult to see. I do not think you can plan too far ahead of provincial Iraqi control; we have to get the plan in place and executed to hand over control of the city, we have to see the consequences of that. If the consequences allow us to move on to provincial control and get that done, then after we see the shape of that we have got to talk to the Iraqi Government and, yes, our Coalition partners about what further contribution they want from us, what further contribution we are capable of making, what they want from us on an ongoing basis, what we can offer going forward. You cannot really have those conversations until you get there, until you see the shape of it and until you see the consequences of handing over that fourth province to the Iraqis.

Q118 Mr Crausby: There is clearly a minimum force level, there cannot be a lot below what we are now and it is that that we are interested in. You clearly cannot drop down by 500, 500, 500 to a point where we are not able to protect our forces, and we must be coming close to that point.
Mr Ainsworth: The force is not self-sustaining and able to protect itself and do the other work that it has to do below about 5000, so we are approaching the levels where we cannot go further.

Q119 Mr Crausby: The Secretary of State said we will then be in a position of over-watch after we have reduced by the 500. The point we are interested in is,

is over-watch that necessary within Iraq itself and to what extent could we provide effective over-watch from outside Iraq, in Kuwait for instance?
Mr Ainsworth: That is what we have got to see.

Q120 Chairman: We would not expect details.
Mr Ainsworth: That is what we are going to have to see and that is what we are going to have to talk about when we see what over-watch is. If it goes as smoothly as the other three provinces then there can be real hope and we can discuss that situation at the time, but until we see what it is—in an actual over-watch situation we cannot get much below 5000 because we have to be able to sustain the force and self-protect the force itself, so over-watch in itself does not take us down a lot lower than that.

Q121 Mr Jones: A simple question; what is over-watch?
Mr Ainsworth: What is over-watch? Over-watch is being there, able in the absolute extreme to offer support, but to stand back and allow the Iraqi Forces themselves to try to deal with the situations that arise.
Chairman: You have been talking about Provincial Iraqi Control, Minister. Willie Rennie.

Q122 Willie Rennie: You have already mentioned that you would hope to achieve Provincial Iraqi Control in the near future, and I can understand why you do not want to be any more precise about that, but why has it been so difficult and would you respond to our concern that the reason why it has not already been achieved is for domestic American purposes rather than the ability of the Iraqi military to be able to cope in the South?
Mr Ainsworth: We are a sovereign nation and there is a process that needs to be gone through in order to get to Provincial Iraqi Control. We have not got sole control of that process, that is true, the Iraqi Government themselves have been part of that, our allies have been part of that, so those discussions have to take place and we have to be part of that. It is not true to say that it is the Americans who are preventing that; the biggest single part of that discussion is the discussion with the Iraqi Security Forces themselves: what is their capacity, what is their capability, are they ready for it? We may be approaching that point where they are.

Q123 Willie Rennie: If we had already achieved the military capability, surely that is the overriding factor rather than the domestic politics of perhaps another country.
Mr Ainsworth: They need to understand as well the consequences of us going to over-watch and what we will and what we will not do. It is no good them accepting provincial control and assuming that we are going to come in and support them on a regular basis because that will not be the situation.
Mr Bowen: Can I just say that there are criteria and some of the criteria that need to be dealt with cannot be dealt with in a completely objective and scientific way. There are four criteria: one is about the security situation, another is about the state of the Iraqi

Security Forces and their ability to cope, another is about the state of governance—in other words the political control and the processes—and the fourth is the ability of the multinational forces to support Provincial Iraqi Control. There are therefore some very clear categories, against which we can report in order to make the case for Provincial Iraqi Control and then there is a process which has been established which involves submitting to Baghdad, and in Baghdad both the Coalition and the Iraqi Government coming together to agree that province X or province Y is ready for transfer. That same process has been applied not just in the South but elsewhere and fairly recently in the North.

Q124 Willie Rennie: You do not believe that domestic US politics were a significant factor in the decision not to transfer already.
Mr Bowen: There is a process. All I can say is there is a process which is Iraq-based, in Baghdad, involving the multinational forces and the Iraqi Government and that is what has determined the PIC of provinces across Iraq.

Q125 Chairman: Can you tell us what the current status of the Governor of Basra is, please?
Mr Ainsworth: Well, he is . . .

Q126 Chairman: It sounds as though the answer is no.
Mr Ainsworth: It is in the public domain and everybody knows that there have been attempts to remove the governor from within the structures within Basra. The Prime Minister himself has said that he should cease to operate and no longer has effective office there; nonetheless he does continue to operate. That is a matter for the Iraqis at the end of the day, we cannot intervene in that, we can only say to the Iraqi Government it is not an aid to stability that they are unable to sort that situation out, they need to get that situation sorted out one way or another and they need to bring clarity to that. It would be a huge help if they did.

Q127 Willie Rennie: Going to the other provinces that have already handed over to PIC, how are they performing in terms of security and politics and what has our role been in those provinces since they were handed over?
Mr Ainsworth: We have not had to intervene.
Brigadier Hughes: We have on a couple of occasions.
Mr Ainsworth: Two of the provinces have been better than the other in terms of the degree of problems that there have been. Maysaan has been the more difficult of the three, but by and large the Iraqis have dealt with those problems themselves. The Brigadier can give you some information on the interventions that we have had to make.
Brigadier Hughes: We will go round clockwise. In Al-Muthanna, which was the first to go, west of Basra, it has been largely peaceful but it is largely desert as well, which is one of the reasons for the peace. It was interesting actually that straight after it gained PIC the Australians, who had been there—along with the Japanese but the Australians were

looking after the security as part of MND (South East)—tried paying an early visit to the governor in Al Muthanna just to check that everything was okay; they were given a pretty quick cold shoulder: we are now looking after this, we no longer require you in Muthanna and, indeed, we have never had to re-intervene there. Dhi Qar has been a little more problematic, particularly recently in An Nasiriyah, the main city in Dhi Qar, where there have been similar sorts of militant JAM versus Iraqi Police Service issues that have been going on in Basra. There was a stand-off there a few weeks ago which the Iraqi Security Forces dealt with, with Coalition support, but when I say "Coalition support" it was air support and ISTAR—that is surveillance and target acquisition assets—rather than boots on the ground. In Maysaan, again, there have been some challenges up there but it is worth saying that actually what is going on in Maysaan is difficult to tell, even when you are there, so some of this is grey to us. There have certainly been issues with militias and the police service in Maysaan; the Iraqis have dealt with that largely themselves and the only intervention there has been into Maysaan Province, again quite recently, over the last two or three weeks, which has been a national operation because even after a province has PIC'd the national government keeps responsibility for terrorism. There was a Coalition operation, a US operation, into Maysaan which Prime Minister Maliki approved and Prime Minister Maliki gave down to there, but we have not re-intervened at provincial level back into Maysaan. The short answer is that there have been one or two blips, as we expected, this is not peace, love and harmony through three provinces, nobody would pretend that, but it has been largely good. Basra, of course, is a different order of issue because of the population, oil, etc.

Q128 Willie Rennie: Relations between the central government and these provinces on terrorism or anything that is reserved to the central government, how are they developing?
Brigadier Hughes: Normally on a mobile phone. It is that, it is the personal relationships that you see out there; if something is going to go off it does need the Prime Minister or his known representative to make a call, it cannot be done in the administrative way that we would recognise here.

Q129 Willie Rennie: Relationships are good?
Brigadier Hughes: They are mixed, and it depends on who is after what at any one time, so you will find that Governor Wa'ili, for example, will quite often say "I need to go and check with Baghdad" and then at other times he will ignore Baghdad, so they shift around depending on who is after what, frankly, but they exist, the relationships exist.

Q130 Mr Jenkin: Just as a supplementary and as a linked question, that sort of Maysaan operation that we have been doing, is that the sort of thing we might continue doing from the position of over-watch after transition?

Brigadier Hughes: It is possible. What we do not envisage in over-watch is one package fits all, so if the Iraqi Security Forces were going to ask us for support once they have got provincial control, we do not envisage them necessarily meaning that we have got to put a battle group into the middle of the city. What they might be short of is intelligence and surveillance assets, so it might be just flying something high up, or it might be another niche capability or a piece of logistics that they need putting in place. We foresee in over-watch maybe nothing or maybe very limited and a scaled approach to it.

Q131 Mr Jenkin: To carry on giving Min(AF) a little rest, could you give us a thumbnail sketch from a military viewpoint, where are the Iraqi Armed Forces now in terms of capability and development, particularly the 10th Division, what more do they need?
Brigadier Hughes: The 10th Division, as I have said, has had some genuine success and we have been pleased and we have had people with them whilst they have had that success, with battalions up in Baghdad and with some operations down in Basra Province and elsewhere in South East Iraq. They do have routine control alongside the police, but largely it is the Army in the three provinces that we have mentioned that have already gone to PIC. They have had effect in some of the operations in Basra; where we have seen difficulty is where the loyalty issue then comes into play and, as I have said, we have been trying to address that. In terms of equipment levels, they are well-equipped at the moment with their frontline kit so they have got 100% of the up-armoured Humvees that they were due to get and their other vehicles and equipment. The British Government has put £54 million through OSIRIS[1] into the Iraqi Security Forces as well as the equipment that has flowed down from Baghdad, originally from the Coalition and now from the Iraqi Ministry of Defence. Where they still lack and we know they still lack is at the rear end; they have not got a big logistics footprint yet, but that was planned, they do lack some of the intelligence assets, but are they a reasonable force, given where they have come from in the timeframe that they have come from, yes they are. Do they have problems? Yes, they do. In terms of the defence border, the Department for Border Enforcement (the DBE) we continue to mentor them. We have seen them make quite impressive strides at some of the key crossing points with the Iran-Iraq border where we have tightened up some of the real issues there, and it was where a lot of the smuggling was going on—it is where some of the smuggling is still going on because you are not going to stop that. They continue to be taken forward and, as I say, we continue with the SSR process on that. The Iraqi Police Service is the biggest challenge; there is no doubt about that and it remains so in Basra. We identified quite a while ago

---

[1] The UK funding support to the Iraqi Security Forces is provided through OPERATION Osiris and to date, around £13m of this has been used to fund support to Iraqi Army 10 Division.

and we have continued to work on this with the Iraqis, on getting the Iraqi Police Service in Basra as best as it can possibly be. Effectively there is a small, murderous, criminal element within the Iraqi Police Force which we have to root out, and indeed we have upped our strike and detention operations against them in recent months in order to do that because they are truly irreconcilable. There are those within the Police Force whom General Jalil, for example, has said recently are totally incompetent and will always be so. If that is the case then we need to drive forward with trying to get them out of the Police Force in some way. Jalil is charged with that and only the Iraqi Government is going to be able to do that, with some sort of resettlement package if you like that is going to keep them quiet once they have gone. The rest are trainable and we continue to train where we can—during Operation SINBAD last year, for example, going into every police station to make sure that certain standards were met and with direct mentoring and support to specialist units such as the CID. We understand, therefore, what a problem the Iraqi Police Service in Basra is, but we are doing what we can to put that right as far as we are able.

Q132 Mr Jenkin: Very briefly, because you have given very comprehensive answers, but two very brief questions, how long is it going to take before we can take our hands off so to speak?
Brigadier Hughes: We do not know. We know that we can continue to do what we can, but to some extent that SSR timeline will not be the driver because you will be driven by other timelines as well about Provincial Iraqi Control, so it is when the Iraqis decide and the Coalition decides that we are ready for transition that you will come to a view then as to what to take forward post-transition into PIC. We have programmes where we can tick off units, but to give you a dead stop time I could not do.

Q133 Mr Jenkin: Concerns that were expressed to us about the Iraqi Government being very slow at their equipment programmes; would you agree with that and can that be addressed?
Brigadier Hughes: It can be addressed. We have people inside the Iraqi MoD—in fact we are putting another procurement specialist in in the next couple of weeks. They have been slow; one of the issues is the anti-corruption law that the Coalition put in place to try and address some of the very serious corruption. That makes people quite frightened to sign contracts, but we do have people in place to try and drive that forward.
Chairman: That struck us as being improved in terms of the Iraqi Government actually procuring equipment over last year. Dai Havard.

Q134 Mr Havard: Within that, however, we had a meeting with the Defence Minister while we were there and he was very clear that General Mohan's appointment in Basra was an important step in unifying command and control for all security assets—that was the euphemism for going in and trying to sort the thing out and give a consistent,

coherent pattern there. The resources he has at his disposal to do that, however, we also discussed that, and it is this 5th Brigade within the 10th Division and this 14th Division that apparently is going to appear and is going to apparently drop out of the sky as far as I am concerned. I have little confidence, frankly, that that is going to come on the timeframe that they were telling us and is going to be equipped—given our experience of 12 months to get to the stage we are with the 10th Division. Can you say something about that because this really relates to how long we are going to stay and what we are going to do, and this business about their capacity there to do it. General Mohan may well be able to knock heads together and accommodate militias and have some architecture of control; however, what resources have you got to actually police it?
Mr Ainsworth: The equipment is there for the existing people, the existing 10th Division.

Q135 Mr Havard: The 10th Division, yes.
Mr Ainsworth: The idea is that they grow the 5th Brigade of 10th Division; they are already part way there, but they are not fully equipped, so they are still in the process of being formed, and then at some stage after that you can effectively split the division and create 14th Division and effect this turnaround that the Brigadier talked about, so that we can get the Basra-based people out of Basra and into the other provinces.

Q136 Mr Havard: It is like the South Wales Police beating up South Wales miners—I have seen it, yes, I know that.
Mr Ainsworth: It is a big job and whether they have got the numbers yet is part of the conversation that we are having.

Q137 Mr Havard: They have not got the equipment, they have not got the capacity, they are not there. They are a fiction.
Mr Ainsworth: At the same time that they are saying that they have not got the numbers and they are attempting to grow their capacity, they are equally beginning to express their confidence in being able to take over in Basra town and being able to take over in the province. We have to balance that conversation, we have to understand that conversation and they have to understand the size of the job they are taking on.

Q138 Mr Havard: The Defence Minister seemed to think they would be there and they would be available by September. I am afraid I do not share his confidence.
Mr Ainsworth: Who will be there by September?

Q139 Mr Havard: The 14th Division.
Mr Ainsworth: I do not think that is the timescale that people are working to but I am not very sure.
Brigadier Hughes: Not everybody is giving the same date. You are right to be sceptical, things do not normally run to time. We have had some people say September at the left hand scale of it; we have heard some say early in the new year, January. Somewhere

in there is probably about right, but the important thing here—and we have genuinely seen signs of this—is the Government recognising the importance of Basra. It is always uppermost in their minds, for perfectly understandable reasons, that Baghdad comes first and so a lot of the equipment flow has gone straight into Baghdad. If there is a genuine belief that Mohan can deliver, and in the importance of Basra, we will see it come on line quicker.

Q140 Chairman: Is the entire purpose of this 14th Division to allow for the stationing of Basra troops out of Basra and other troops into Basra, or is that not?
Mr Ainsworth: It is a big part of it, whether it is the only part I am not too sure.
Brigadier Hughes: It is not the sole reason, Chairman. The reason was that there was a recognition that were not enough army battalions in the province and elsewhere in MND (South East), but it is a pretty key side effect for us that we now are able to do that.

Q141 Chairman: Can I ask when you first heard of this 14th Division?
Brigadier Hughes: Yes, two or three months ago. That is from my memory but it is about that sort of time scale as to when it was being put forward.
Mr Havard: I have to raise a question with you, which is in my head: I look at Anbar and that is a question of having local resources there take control locally, and trying to then assimilate them into the normal forces of Iraq and the national Army process. I am just wondering, in terms of actually winning that capacity in Basra, whether or not Mohan has to do that sort of exercise, because I do not see this capacity coming from anywhere else on the timescale that they are talking about and, more importantly, which chimes back into the point that was being made earlier on, how long we can stay and how long apparently we can afford to stay. It is a rhetorical question.
Chairman: Let us assume that is rhetorical and move on to the police.

Q142 Willie Rennie: You have actually greatly covered some of my questions; I just have another couple. You did not mention much about the militias in Basra but there is quite a significant militia infiltration. Some people view it as being reasonably stable, even if they only patrol their own areas and protect their own circumstance. How do you deal with that, do you accept that or what method is there to try and root out the inappropriate lines of accountability here?
Mr Ainsworth: This harks back to some of the questions we were talking about, about what General Mohan is up to in some of the conversations that he is having. What is the raison d'etre of some of the militias, even some of those that may be attacking us, what is their motive, what are they up to, are they winnable, are they fundamentally prepared to support the Iraqi state at some point? If so they are worth talking to and they are worth trying to win over. If they are totally maligned, for

whatever reason, supporting corrupt political processes or with a political motive that is totally contrary to the well-being of the country, then they are not. Getting that understanding, seeing who can win and who cannot win, is an important part of what has got to go on. On top of that, coming back to the rhetorical point, you have to try to get effective forces into the area and if they are being intimidated because their families live alongside these elements of the JAM and they are unable to operate, then commanders have to try and deal with that. If they can deal with that by rotation then they are going to do so.

Q143 Willie Rennie: If the UK Forces were to withdraw could our police trainers still be there to support the police; would that be something that would be safe?
Mr Ainsworth: We do some of the training out in the COB. The further we withdraw then the more difficult it is for us to operate. If we see a transformed situation, if we see a new attitude, then we will have that ability, but potentially it is going to be more difficult, is it not?
Chairman: We touched earlier on the surge, but let us get back to that in a bit more detail now. Bernard Jenkin.

Q144 Mr Jenkin: I am bound to preface my question by pointing out that we did get very diverse opinions on whether the surge was the right thing or the wrong thing from the British military, underlining a point made by Mr Jones, and I would say the British military is very divided and publicly divided. Would you recognise that that is a problem that you are inheriting in terms of the capacity of the Armed Forces to deliver, that some of the Armed Forces are campaigning for Britain to get out whilst some are trying to succeed in what they are doing. Do you recognise that as a problem?
Mr Ainsworth: There may be scepticism about whether or not the surge will succeed, but it is too early—

Q145 Mr Jenkin: My question was really about the state of the morale of our Armed Forces.
Mr Ainsworth: Our Armed Forces.

Q146 Mr Jenkin: Yes, which are divided, with some branches of the Armed Forces actively campaigning to get us out of Iraq as quickly as possible because of the overstretch. Do you actually recognise that that is a problem?
Mr Ainsworth: I saw no evidence of morale problems.

Q147 Mr Jenkin: Not in Iraq, the problem is back home.
Mr Ainsworth: As a matter of fact I was surprised by the high morale that there is there.

Q148 Mr Jenkin: So were we, we were very impressed, but back home in the Ministry of Defence.

Mr Ainsworth: They were upbeat there, doing the job that they joined the Army to do and there is not a morale problem there at all.

Q149 Mr Jenkin: I totally agree with that, but in the Ministry of Defence you are inheriting a very big problem with some senior military officers actively almost campaigning publicly to get us out, at the same time as other branches of the Armed Forces are desperately trying to succeed. Is that not really a result of a long period of protracted overstretch which is what General Dannatt was referring to?
Mr Ainsworth: You know that I am new to the department.

Q150 Mr Jenkin: I know.
Mr Ainsworth: My impression is that there is—and this is out there as well—an intelligent conversation going on about how long we can continue to do the things that we can do, how important it is to hand on that job to the Iraqis themselves, and it is right that people discuss those issues and examine those issues, and that is taking place. We are at this transition point, as the Brigadier said, which is an enormously difficult position.
Chairman: We will move on to the Surge, please.

Q151 Mr Jenkin: We heard some very positive assessment of the Surge, but perhaps I could ask the Brigadier, would you not agree that the Surge is really about increased manoeuvrability and capability, it is not a policy, an end in itself?
Brigadier Hughes: There have been a number of successes that have come from the Surge. The figures for vehicle-borne IEDs are down; the figures for murders of civilians are significantly down. It is true to say that that additional security that has come in Baghdad has not just been displaced somewhere else; in some of the other provinces AQI in particular is being given a hard time, but I do not think that General Petraeus ever said that the Surge was an end in itself, what he was trying to do was to give some time for the politics to breathe. Also, there are two measures which people will be looking closely at which we do not have a feel for yet fully: to what extent the breathing space that the military surge has given in the security situation—and I think it has—has allowed the politics to breathe, and to what extent are the Iraqi Security Forces able to back up what has largely been this Coalition surge. Those are the two questions which remain unanswered as of today.

Q152 Mr Jenkin: Could you say something that we heard a little about, which is the rewriting of the campaign plan for the Coalition, putting politics at the top of the agenda as opposed to merely the suppression of violence, because this was a very positive development?
Brigadier Hughes: I can say very little about it because I saw only little of it when I was last in Baghdad two or three weeks ago. It is being rewritten, it is not yet out. I do not know any senior officer in Baghdad on the military side who does not

understand that it is about politics, not about security; everybody gets that a bit of it is security, but people do get the bigger piece.

Q153 Linda Gilroy: In that context, Minister, what significance do you attach to the recent White House report which concluded that there had been satisfactory progress on only 8 of the 18 benchmarks which were set out?
Mr Ainsworth: It was only an interim report and, you are right, the amount of progress that could be reported was partial. I do not think there are too many conclusions that can be drawn yet on whether or not the Surge has had the success that people hoped it would, and we really will have to wait for the report that will be made in September and the assessment that will be done then.

Q154 Linda Gilroy: The report sets out a variety of benchmarks, some of which are to do with creating security and what might be described as leading indicators, whereas some of the other things, the things that have not been met, include things like satisfactory legislation for de-Ba'athification, hydrocarbon resources, provincial law, an amnesty law, and it is on the whole those more political ones that are not being met. Those might be described more as lagging indicators that will take more time to achieve—the sort of breathing space that Chris Hughes referred to just now. Do you think, therefore, that the benchmarks set out a realistic set of indicators on which we should be judging things, our allies should be judging things, come September?
Mr Ainsworth: You are right that the politics are potentially the area that is lagging, and if we do not get some agreement on hydrocarbons then the ability of the Iraqis to build trust across the various regions and across the communities is going to be damaged, so those political benchmarks plus a real reaching out to the Sunni community are essential, otherwise all of the effort that has been made during the surge will not have that backfill.

Q155 Linda Gilroy: Do you have any sense from your experience thus far of how far the Iraqi Government is successfully moving to bridging the sectarian divide?
Mr Ainsworth: I do not yet; I did not manage to get up there, as I said, and I have not really got a good handle on how far progress is being made there.

Q156 Linda Gilroy: Is it perhaps something that Desmond could comment on?
Mr Bowen: Chairman, actually from the beginning when the Surge was first announced the intention was to put politics and indeed economics in the frontline and, through better security, to provide an opportunity for Iraqis to take charge of their own destiny and make politics work and indeed make economics operate in a way that would be helpful overall but, not least, helpful in showing that the Iraqis could take charge of their own destiny in that way. What we would say is that reconciliation and the whole business of politics in Iraq has been slower and more complicated than we would like; that is

very much the area where we would like to see good progress and it is fair to say that we are disappointed that things are not moving forward more quickly. The hydrocarbons law is an absolute classic in terms of the interaction of economics and politics, and that is something on which some progress has been made but it has not got to the point where it is resolved. The same can be said on some of the other issues. You talked about de-Ba'athification in the same way, amnesty, likewise on the provincial election law; is this happening as fast as we would like? No, it certainly is not. Is there cause to despair? That is something that we really cannot afford to do and we really need to be, on the political side, pushing forward—not just us and Coalition partners but the wider international community to encourage the Iraqis to do the things that need to be done in both politics and economics.

Q157 Linda Gilroy: I spent some time with the British-American Parliamentary Group over in the States just last week, and there seems to be very much a public perception in the States that the benchmarks are about military success rather than the political breathing space which has been created which may take a little longer to take root in the space that has been created. Do you think that there is a danger that there will be too much emphasis placed on assessing the military benchmarks rather than giving that space for the political benchmarks to have the time that they need to take root, and is there anything that we can do to influence that?
Mr Bowen: The 18 benchmarks were set out by Congress, so clearly very much in a political context and in a political context of some tension between the executive and the legislature.

Q158 Linda Gilroy: And the Presidential race of course, and that is something which may not be so apparent over here in the United Kingdom, that the assessment of the benchmarks now and in September are very much subject to people seeking political advantage basically.
Mr Bowen: I am sure that is the case. What the American Government, in particular Ambassador Crocker and General Petraeus, have to do in presenting their view from Baghdad, is to be putting it in the right sort of context and making the right sort of balance between, as it were, the buying time and the political and economic progress. That is no doubt something that will be judged in the White House and we will be having contact with the Americans in the process.

Q159 Chairman: Before you leave the benchmarks I have a question, then Bernard Jenkin has a question, then we will come back to you. My question is do you have a sense, Mr Bowen, that the very setting of benchmarks by Western timescales, possibly to some sort of US political advantage, goes down badly in Iraq and leads to a process where they are bound to come up in some way with some sort of rather unsatisfactory result?

Mr Bowen: I cannot speak for how it is taken in Baghdad, my only comment on as it were the 18 benchmarks is that they were selected. They could have been a different set, they could have been longer or they could have been different. As I say, there is a political context in that which we have to recognise is there, but whether they are the optimal means of making objective judgment I will not comment.

Q160 Mr Jenkin: Is there not a much clearer message we should be conveying about these benchmarks—and maybe this is one for the Minister—in that first of all they provide an easy target for the insurgents and the terrorists to stop us achieving. Secondly, many of them are irrelevant. Frankly, the rights of minority parties in the legislature is not a top military priority or a top political priority; winning the hearts and minds of Sunni tribal leaders I would say is a massively important priority, but it is not one of the benchmarks. Is this not a rubbish way of organising a counter-insurgency campaign and would not the President be pleased if the British Government said it loudly and clearly?
Mr Ainsworth: The benchmarks have been made and the process has started. We will have to see what comes out of it in September.
Chairman: What a brilliant answer. Linda Gilroy.

Q161 Linda Gilroy: I am particularly interested if Mr Bowen has any further comments on the bridging of the sectarian divide and one of the benchmarks which has not been met in the interim report, which is on moving towards de-Ba'athification law, and also whether there is any up to date information about the questions we were asking in January, that is the release of the Sunni detainees and whether the Iraqi Government are moving towards that. If you have not got information to hand perhaps you would let the Committee have an update on the situation because that is seen as very much symbolic of the Maliki Government doing something which it does have within its control, which would show goodwill in that respect.
Mr Bowen: Chairman, we ought to give you a note on that.[2] The one thing I would say in terms of recent developments is that the withdrawal some months ago of the large Sunni block from the Council of Representatives was reversed in recent days, so they have now reverted as it were to being part of that assembly. How has that come about? By way of a long and difficult process of political negotiation involving the Prime Minister and the Shia parties operating together to try and bring them back into the fold. It is not as though politics is not happening, but it is a very complex, convoluted and long drawn-out process, so it is worth saying that there is some movement but I do not think that that equals reconciliation.

Q162 Willie Rennie: There has been much said about the tribal reawakening in Anbar Province, but do you not think we should be quite cautious because it is just one province, we do not know how long it is

[2] See Ev 35

going to last, and we do not know whether we can replicate that in other parts of the country? What is your view on the tribal reawakening?

Mr Ainsworth: There has got to be a silent hope. There is an indication that the people themselves, on the ground, object to al-Qaeda, in particular, in this case, so there has to be a silent hope. Whether we can draw too many conclusions from that that are going to be applicable in different parts of the country has yet to be seen. Tribal structures in the more rural areas are a lot stronger than they are in the cities, where there is an altogether different dynamic that goes on. We should not dismiss it.

Q163 Willie Rennie: We met Petraeus when we were out there and I was very impressed then; I thought he was very competent. I had the feeling, though— and I am trying not to be a bit like *Dad's Army*: "We're all doomed!"—that the die was cast and that we were kind of going through the motions for the political domestic agenda back in the States, and that really progress was not going to be significantly made in the timescales that had been talked about.

Mr Ainsworth: I have not met Petraeus yet, so I have not been able to get a handle. My visit was confined to south-east Iraq.

Q164 Chairman: Can we move on to the issue of Iran? Can you give us a brief assessment of the extent of Iranian influence in Iraq?

Mr Ainsworth: The influence is quite strong. It is long-standing. There have always been close relationships, particularly in the south; there are people who live on both sides of the border who choose not to recognise the border, and that has been so for a very long time. There is clear evidence of malign influence across the border in the Basra area. There is little doubt, when you look at some of the munitions that are being used against our people, to kill our people, they are not being made in garages in down-town Basra; they are coming from outside the area. We hope that the Iranians will take seriously the need for their active engagement in the area and their active effort to prevent the kind of things that are very, very clearly happening. It cannot be in Iran's long-term interests that we have got chaos and instability on their border; it has got to be more important to them in many ways than it is to us. We have got to use our efforts to try to convince the Iranian Government that that is the case and that they could do a lot more. It is certainly the feeling of our people on the ground that there is lots of activity coming across the border, there is lots of effective support being given and there needs to be more effort to control it.

Q165 Chairman: So, clearly, you have the sense that the Iranians are fuelling the violence. Do you think that that would continue were multinational forces to leave the MND (South-East) area?

Mr Ainsworth: I do not think it would necessarily end. It might (and this is one of the things that General Mohan says) help him to be able to focus the minds of the Iraqi Shia in Basra themselves as to where their loyalties ought to lie, because most of them are loyal to the Iraqi State; they are fundamentally nationalist in their outlook. Therefore, if it gives him more space, if he is able to say: "Right, the British have pulled out of Basra Palace, there is no British presence in our city now"—if he is able to say that to elements of the militia and able to say: "What's your excuse for the continuing violence" then that might give him the ability to make some progress in some of the dynamics he is trying to achieve on the ground.

Q166 Chairman: The Iraq Commission suggests that the UK should seek to promote the constructive engagement of Iraq's neighbours. Does that mean that you should be talking, do you think, to the Iranian Government?

Mr Ainsworth: I think we should talk to the Iranian Government. It is essential that we talk to the Iranian Government, but I think it is important that the Iraqi Government talks to the Iranian Government as well, and that they build a strong relationship. It is one of the most key relationships in the area, so Iranians can be a force for good. They can also create a huge problem, and that problem is not going to benefit them in the long-term. Whether they see it that way I am not at all sure, but dialogue would do us no harm whatsoever.

Q167 Mr Havard: That leads me on to the question about the United Nations, because I agree with all of that and I think the question of how you incentivise the neighbours in a constructive way to help solve the problem is a huge discussion. Quite clearly, the military utility of what we are doing is coming to an end and, therefore, the politics need to be taken forward. I just love the whole thing, Desmond, about the benchmarks not being an "optimal" way and Bernard's contrast of "it's a pile of rubbish"! He has obviously cancelled his subscription to the American Enterprise Institute's journals now, which is a good thing.

Mr Ainsworth: That was not what he was trying to achieve! I did not read it that way, anyway.

Mr Jenkin: It was congressional benchmarks.

Q168 Mr Havard: Yes, written by the American Enterprise Institute. The criteria by which all these things are going to be judged in terms, however, is not just in America; it is going to be in the United Nations because, at the moment, we have a coalition of the willing, essentially, prosecuting a UN mandate to help to do two things in Iraq: help the Iraqis and, also, fight al-Qaeda. The Americans see it as part of, whatever it is—the War on Terror, or whatever. So there is confusion, and that confusion will reflect itself within the UN in the renewal of the mandate discussions before the end of the calendar year, which are of crucial importance not least to us because it gives us a legitimacy there both domestically in politics but, also, practically, on the ground for things like running detention centres and so on. So how is it going to be internationalised— and it is going to be highly politicised? Can I just raise a question: it is not all going to run on the timetable of the renewal of the next President of

America; there is a debate that is going to involve beyond the coalition of the willing and the Iraqi Government at that point. What is going to happen in terms of the renewal of that UN mandate discussion before the end of the calendar year? Without it what are we going to do then? If we do not get it are we going to come out?

Mr Ainsworth: I am sorry, Dai, I am struggling to understand what the question is. The question is: do we need a renewed mandate? Yes, we do. Can we operate without one? No, we cannot. So we are operating, as are the Americans, under a UN mandate that runs out on 31 December and we need a new mandate. All the rest of it is politics, is it not? We have our own politics to deal with, the Americans have their politics to deal with—that is not going to change. However, we need a new UN mandate and we need that renewed on the 31st.[3]

Q169 Chairman: What will be the factors in helping to decide whether we get it?

Mr Ainsworth: I would suppose the factors are going to be the UN's view of what can be achieved ongoing, the necessity for our continued presence and the continued powers that they have effectively given us. I do not know what more I can say, other than those ought to be the factors.

Mr Havard: Can I ask you a direct question? In a sense, if General Mohan is successful, if the economic engine of the country, which is the South East, is helped to be secured—all the attention at the moment is about the nihilistic violence in Baghdad—is it not the case that, in fact, these questions about what happens in the South East are actually probably going to become more important in determining what comes out of that process (or equally) than some of the things that are happening in Baghdad?

Q170 Chairman: That is a "Yes" or "No" question.

Mr Ainsworth: A big part of the renewal process is going to be the Iraqi Government and whether or not they see the need for renewal and the method of renewal. If they want us to continue to do the job that we are doing they are going to have to support renewal. We hope they do see the necessity for that.

Q171 Mr Havard: How we configure ourselves and what we do in that intervening period—whether it is withdraw troops, come down, move out—is taking on a different significance, is it not?

Mr Ainsworth: I think that is not what is steering our policy at the moment. What is steering our policy at the moment is our assessment of the situation on the ground in the South East and whether or not we are in a position to hand over control of that fourth

province to the Iraqis. That is at the forefront. Everybody I talk to—that is what they are focused on.

Chairman: This is obviously a matter of great importance to us.

Mr Havard: And General Dannatt's assessment of whether it will "break" the Army.

Q172 Mr Jenkins: Minister, some simple questions on equipment. How are the new Mastiffs performing in theatre? Do you rate them?

Mr Ainsworth: I had an opportunity to have a look at them and talk to the people who were using them. They appear to be a pretty impressive piece of kit to me, but, more importantly, the people who are actually using them have a high degree of confidence in them; they like what they have been given; they feel that there is a level of security there that is fitting to the job that they are being asked to do. So, yes, they are very, very enthusiastic about not only the Mastiff but the Bulldog as well.

Q173 Mr Jenkins: Do we have enough of them?

Mr Ainsworth: Every army would always like more, but we have got this new kit into the field pretty quickly. I think that is recognised out there. Certainly we are able to use it for the operations that are necessary.

Q174 Mr Jenkins: Every army wants more, as you said, but there is a need to make sure they are provided with enough to do the job.

Mr Ainsworth: Yes.

Q175 Mr Jenkins: We can replace the soft-skin vehicles with these vehicles when they are appropriate. So we have to make sure there are enough of them.

Mr Ainsworth: Outside of those who involve themselves in these issues there is a notion that there is a "one size fits all" and that certain of our vehicles are beyond their sell-by date and have to be replaced in their entirety. Now, as I have had explained to me over the last few weeks and graphically on the ground by the people who are doing these operations, that is not the case; they configure the operations with the kit that they have got and they use the appropriate vehicles in the appropriate circumstances. So when we are sending convoys into Basra there is still a need for Land Rovers to get in among the small streets in the city itself, but they are not the front line of the approach. The convoy is constructed in order to do the job that it is there to do. People feel—or they certainly said to me—that they have the equipment to do that; they are able to successfully get into the city, but, yes, they are still using snatch vehicles, and they are needed for certain operations.

Q176 Mr Jenkins: That was a full answer, Minister. Very often when people talk a lot we have to go back and have a look at what they are saying. I did ask you: do we have enough? What I wanted to make sure is that we are not configuring for the equipment we have got, we are configuring for the job we are

---

[3] Note by Witness: We believe that, given the current tasks and responsibilities of the Coalition in Iraq, a UN Security Council resolution provides the most appropriate legal framework and international legitimacy for the Coalition's presence in Iraq. But should those tasks and responsibilities change or a different international political climate emerge, we and our Coalition partners could seek an alternative legal mechanism, with the agreement with the Iraqi Government, to enable our forces to remain in Iraq and operate effectively according to a revised sets of tasks and responsibilities.

trying to undertake. Whilst we accept the Army has a long tradition of "putting up and doing with" equipment I want to be sure that we are not exposing them to any greater risk than their normal job entails by saying: "Yes, we do have enough, we believe, in theatre at the present time".

Mr Ainsworth: What I got when I was out there was an enormous amount of pleasure at the amount of new equipment that had been provided over the period of time. People were very pleased at what had been got to them. If you ask them whether or not they could do with some more, I am certain that they would say that they could.

Mr Jenkins: You say the amount of equipment we have got there is very appreciable. Good, because we had a lot of trouble with our urgent operational requirements procedure, did we not, to start with? It took a few months before we could get up to speed. Are we satisfied now that it is performing effectively? Before you tell me it is (which I would expect, at any rate) would you like to send us a note on how you assess and evaluate the effectiveness of it, how it was operating 18 months or two years ago and what improvements have been made since then, so we can actually see a quantifiable assessment of how effective it has become.[4]

Chairman: This is the UORs?

Q177 Mr Jenkins: Yes.

Mr Ainsworth: Just because we are able to raise a UOR and raise a UOR in pretty short order does not mean to say that, hey presto, off the shelf is the stuff that we want there and available immediately. Various stuff has to be procured, it has to be found and it has to be bought and shipped out to theatre. Everything that I am being told is that that process is running reasonably smoothly and that we are able to get the kit out to our people that they need. Everything I saw on the ground was that they have the kit they need; that there has been a big improvement over a period of time and they are very satisfied with the progress that has been made.

Q178 Mr Jenkins: As I said, that is the answer you would give me—I knew that would be the answer.
Mr Ainsworth: So why did you ask!

Q179 Mr Jenkins: The question I asked you is: I believe the situation has improved, but how do you, as a department, evaluate the performance of raising these orders and delivering them, and how has it improved over time? That is all I am asking. If there has been an improvement you must be able to say with confidence it has delivered—prove it in figures. That is what I am asking, so I would be very grateful for a note.
Mr Ainsworth: You would like some figures?
Mr Jenkins: Yes. The next one is helicopter availability.

[4] See Ev 36

Q180 Chairman: Before you move on to helicopters, Minister, when we were in Basra a couple of weeks ago we were told that the senior officers there were very satisfied indeed with the equipment that they had had.
Mr Ainsworth: I got exactly the same.
Mr Jenkins: Did you want to congratulate the—
Chairman: I just wanted to repeat what we had been told.

Q181 Mr Jenkins: I made no assertion as to any different! Proof of the helicopter availability. We get constant comments about the fact that we have a shortage of helicopter availability, which is denied by the Department. How does the Department evaluate the helicopter availability we have got? It must be a concern to them that we are using up our equipment at a far faster rate than was envisaged when we first purchased them. There must be other purchases in the pipeline. How many helicopters do we need to replace the ones we have burned out now? What is available? Can you do us an assessment of the availability on demand rather than the availability monitored by the amount of crews we have got, by the amount of helicopters we have got, or by the maintenance regime it has to undertake? What is the gap between those three and the actual demand required by our services?
Mr Ainsworth: The first thing to say is that forces out in operating areas have the first call on resources. Of the helicopters we have got, obviously, we want the maximum number out there, in the field, supporting our troops. However, that does lead to pressures elsewhere and does mean: do we have sufficient kit at home to maintain adequate training programmes to bring on crews, and the rest of it? So it is not as simple as: do the troops in Iraq have enough helicopters? There are all kinds of other pressures. If you want us to do a note on that then we will give you a note. Pressures do arise in other areas, not necessarily in the operating—

Q182 Mr Jenkins: I did not think it was simple; I think it is very, very complex and very difficult.
Mr Ainsworth: I thought you said you were asking simple questions!

Q183 Mr Jenkins: I will tell you one thing: never listen to a politician. If you tell me that we are holding helicopters back for training in this country and denying our frontline troops the use of helicopters, then that would be a most serious—I do not think you meant that at all.
Mr Ainsworth: That is not what I am telling you at all; I am saying that the pressures on the helicopter fleet tend to come out in areas other than the operating area. That is our first priority, and meeting their needs is the first priority. That means that we wind up with problems elsewhere—which should not be denied. On an ongoing basis, the ability to continue to train and to bring people on is important.

Mr Jenkins: Of course, and if you can give us a note on that we would be very grateful.[5]

Q184 Chairman: Minister, these are questions to which I do not expect you to have an answer because I did not give you any prior warning of them. Last year we travelled in Warriors into Basra Palace and the heat in those Warriors was quite phenomenal. We were told last year that the medical personnel out there were extremely concerned that there would be a heat related fatality that was nothing to do with enemy action. This year we met the helicopter crews that manned the casualty evacuations. They told us that they had had a lot of work to do relating to heat casualties. I wonder whether there is some trade-off between the amount of money that one could spend on putting some air conditioning into some of the vehicles that we are providing compared with the cost of evacuating people through heat related casualties, quite apart from the fact that the better conditions we put our Armed Forces into the better management of people there would be and the fairer it would be to the people who are putting their lives on the line on a daily basis. I wonder if you could do us something, when you answer the questions from Brian Jenkins, about that.

Mr Ainsworth: Okay.[6]

Chairman: I do not know whether there are any further questions. There will be some questions that we want to ask you in writing about detainees, because there are some very important issues we want to pursue on that. No further questions. Then the session is over. Many thanks.

---

[5] See Ev 36

[6] See Ev 36

Written evidence

Supplementary memorandum from the Ministry of Defence

A note on the current situation on detainees, including the numbers detained by US and UK forces, the processes governing detention by UK forces, the release of Sunni detainees by the Iraqi Government, and the prospects for passing responsibility for detention of Iraqi civilians to local Iraqi control. (Q 161)

A note explaining the arrangements for the detention of Iraqi civilians in MND(SE) and why this is still necessary.

UK DETENTION[1] AND INTERNMENT IN IRAQ

Any individual *detained* by UK forces will have his case reviewed by the Divisional Internment Review Committee (DIRC, see below) within 48 hours of initial detention and a decision as to whether internment is necessary will be taken. Individuals are only interned where the DIRC judges that they pose an imperative threat to security.

UK internees are held in the purpose-built Divisional Internment Facility (DIF) at Basra Air Station. As at the end of July 2007, the UK held 86 individuals at the DIF, of which: one has been convicted by the Central Criminal Court of Iraq (CCCI) and is awaiting transfer to the Iraqi Authorities; 10 are awaiting trial in the CCCI; and 75 are security internees.

US INTERNMENT IN IRAQ

At mid-August 2007, the US held around 20,000 internees in their in-theatre internment facilities in Iraq. Further enquiries on US internment policy should be directed to the US authorities.

THE LEGAL BASIS FOR INTERNMENT

The United Nations Security Council Resolution (UNSCR) 1546 (2004) and letters annexed, as continued by subsequent resolutions, provides the legal authority under which Coalition forces may intern individuals "where necessary for imperative reasons of security". Such reasons of security include threats to the security of the Iraqi people as well as to Coalition forces. UK forces comply with all applicable international law obligations when conducting detention operations and subsequent internment.

The overarching practice and procedures following an arrest are enshrined in Iraqi law, namely, Coalition Provisional Authority Memorandum No 3 (Revised).

CRIMINAL DETAINEES AND THEIR TRANSFER TO IRAQI AUTHORITIES

The small number of criminal detainees held by the UK are held in the DIF for and on behalf of the Iraqi authorities. A Criminal Detainee will be released from the DIF if he is placed on bail by the judge presiding over the case. This is often the case where the trial is for a minor offence (these are offences that attract a custodial sentence of three years or less) such as unlawful possession of weapons or low-level theft. In those circumstances, he will return home and be required to attend the Basra Courts at a later date for trial.

Where there is a credible evidential case to answer against an *internee* at the DIF, we look to transfer him to the Iraqi criminal justice system. There is no legal bar to the UK transferring individuals from the DIF to the Iraqi authorities if they are convicted criminals or are held on remand on behalf of the Iraqis, save where there is a real risk that that particular individual may be subject to ill treatment such as torture or arbitrary execution. If a Criminal Detainee has been charged with a serious offence, such as murder or terrorism, then he can not be bailed under Iraqi law. He will therefore remain in the DIF until his trial date. If convicted at trial and given a custodial sentence, he will be held in the DIF until appropriate arrangements have been made to transfer him to Iraqi custody.

The UK takes its responsibilities towards its internees very seriously. To that end, the UK has entered into a Memorandum of Understanding with the Government of Iraq to secure assurances that anyone transferred from UK to Iraqi custody will be treated in accordance with basic international human rights principles.

---

[1] We adopt the following definitions, for clarity:
- "Detention" is defined as the period during which a person is held by MNF following arrest, until he is either transferred to the Iraqi judicial system, or released, or a decision is made by MNF to hold him as an internee.
- "Internment" by MNF refers to the longer-term holding of an individual where it is judged that this is necessary for imperative reasons of security.

INTERNMENT REVIEW PROCEDURES

The coalition's legal obligations regarding internee review, and the review procedures we adopt to meet these obligations, were outlined in the Department's supplementary memorandum of 1 February 2007. There have been no changes to the obligations or review procedures since that time.

SUNNI RELEASES

We are not currently aware of Iraqi plans to pursue an agreement to release some of the individuals currently held in Iraqi prisons. In some contexts, however, the reconciliation process can be promoted through agreements to release prisoners, where this represents part of a wider, agreed framework.

PASSING RESPONSIBILITY FOR INTERNMENT TO THE IRAQI AUTHORITIES

Security internment by Coalition forces is permitted under UNSCR 1723. There is no basis in Iraqi law to allow the Iraqi authorities to undertake such security internment, and new Iraqi legislation would be required if the Iraqis were to take on this power. We have no plans to support such a move, and we do not believe that the Government of Iraq wishes to take on powers of security internment.

WHY INTERNMENT IS STILL NECESSARY

Internment remains necessary because there are still individuals in Iraq whose aim is to undermine the establishment of democratic rule through violence directed at MNF, the Iraqi Security Forces and Iraqi civilians. Internment is used sparingly and only when individuals present an imperative threat to security. Additionally, we need to continue to hold those who have perpetrated attacks against us in the past and who we believe remain a threat to security. Further, internment is in the interest of the Iraqi civilian population and is for their protection as well as our own.

A note on how the Department assesses the performance and effectiveness of the Urgent Operational Requirement (UOR) procurement process, including an assessment (with a breakdown in figures) of how that process is performing now as compared with two years ago, how it has improved over time, and what specific improvements have been made to the UOR system. (Q 176)

The National Audit Office and the Public Accounts Committee have acknowledged the effectiveness of the UOR process at rapidly delivering to the front line the battle-winning capability required by our Armed Forces.

The Department assesses the performance and effectiveness of the Urgent Operational Requirement (UOR) procurement process by conducting a performance effectiveness review. One year after business case endorsement, the relevant Director of Equipment Capability (DEC) raises a capability feedback form which is sent to the equipment cell in the relevant operational theatre, the Front Line Command (FLC), and PJHQ for input. Upon receiving the completed form, the DEC adds its own comments and then feeds this back into the central UOR database. These Capability Reviews form the basis of consideration on bringing particular UOR equipments into core.

As of August 2007, 91% of all equipment procured under the UOR process was deemed either highly effective or effective by troops in Theatre. Of the capability reviews that have been completed and recorded for Op TELIC, 90% were assessed as highly effective or effective. The remainder were deemed as either of limited effectiveness or not used, due predominantly to the changing nature of operations. Of the UORs reviewed for Op HERRICK, 86% were deemed as highly effective, the rest being assessed as effective. The manner in which the Capability Review data is stored means that we are not presently able to produce a discrete snapshot for two years ago. However, DSTL recently conducted an analysis of UORs, which was briefed to the Equipment Capability Area's Joint Capability Board in July 2007. This analysis was conducted on UOR data from January 2005 to March 2007 which determined that from the Endorsement Date to the Into Service Date 50% of UORs are delivered within 6.5 months, 25% within 9.5 months and 15% within 13.5 months (the majority of those within the 13.5 month bracket are highly complex technical integration project UORs eg Defensive Aid Suites onto aircraft). DSTL concluded that: there are no differences in process performance between both operations; that lower cost UORs are not processed more quickly and despite the significant increase in UORs that have been delivered to both theatres there has been no evident delay in the process. In total the Department has now delivered in excess of 450 UORs to Op TELIC and HERRICK.

Further recent improvements to the UOR process include the introduction of a three weekly basis UOR working group to review the progress on all extant UORs. In addition regular video conferences between Theatre Equipment Cells, PJHQ and the equipment capability staffs in main building are conducted. A recent two star end to end business process review for UORs was conducted involving all stakeholders and yielded a number of opportunities, which are now being pursued, for further process performance improvements: for example, improved guidance and training for business case-writers; updated integration guidance for FLCs; and enhanced monitoring of equipment performance in theatre. The SRO also conducts periodic reviews of all longer standing UOR business cases. HQ LAND are leading on work to assist the equipment capability area deliver integrated UOR capability in a more effective manner, drawing on IPT, industry and FLC experience in delivering complex UORs. Defence Equipment and Support (DE&S) have recently formed a UOR cell to improve Board-level visibility of IPT performance in delivering UORs, and to share best practice across the organisation. The cell is currently leading a study on how the DE&S can deliver UORs more effectively to enable increased high level scrutiny of UOR delivery timelines thereby ensuring that delays are quickly highlighted.

A note outlining how the Department evaluates helicopter availability, including details of whether the UK is using up its helicopters at a faster rate than envisaged when they were purchased, what additional helicopter orders are planned, and the pressures on helicopter crew. (Q 181–183)

The primary parameter by which the Department evaluates rotary wing availability is through the delivery of required *flying hours*.[2] Annual flying rates for peacetime flying are set during the Departmental planning round, based on the military outputs required. This includes operational exercises, aircrew currency plus training. The outcome is articulated in the Customer Supplier Agreements (CSAs) between Defence Equipment and Support (DE&S) and the Front Line Commands (FLCs). Monthly flying rates for deployed operations are established taking account of the operational requirement, the number of crews available and on what is sustainable. A balance has to be struck between meeting the immediate operational imperative and the longer-term sustainability of that flying rate. Helicopter availability against CSA and operational flying requirements is reviewed on a monthly basis such that appropriate management action can be taken where necessary.

Most helicopters have a maximum design life based on flying hours that governs useful life of the aircraft, or the rate at which the equipment is "used up".[3] Fleets are therefore managed carefully to ensure that flying hours are accumulated evenly so that the required number of helicopters reach the declared Out of Service Date.

There are a number of factors considered due to the higher utilisation of helicopters on operations:

— *High flying hours on Deployed Helicopters.* When a new operation commences, helicopters will usually require Theatre-specific modifications to be fitted before they deploy. Only a proportion of the fleet are generally modified to Theatre Entry Standard (TES). Flying rates in Theatre tend to be higher than those on routine operations, so deployed helicopters will accumulate flying hours at a higher rate than those not deployed. Left unchecked over a prolonged period, this *may* cause deployed helicopters to reach the end of their fatigue lives early. The Department would, in such circumstances, seek funding for additional helicopters to be modified to mitigate fleet management pressures.[4]

— *Environmental damage.* The conditions experienced in present Theatres can cause damage (ie sand erosion etc) that would not arise in more benign operating environments. This leads to an increase wear rate on key components and an increase in the work required to restore helicopters during Depth maintenance, but will rarely impact on the life of helicopters. Our immediate focus is on work to sustain current operations (eg replacement rotor blades, engines and windscreens).

— *Accidental damage and Attrition.* Enemy action and the increased hazards encountered on Operations can cause the attrition rate to be higher than normal. When the size of the Departmental fleet is comparatively large relative to the number of helicopters required on operations (eg Lynx), such losses can be absorbed. Where the size of the Departmental fleet is smaller (eg Chinook/Puma), it could be necessary to procure replacement helicopters. If attrition rates were to rise significantly then it could become a concern.

While all helicopters have residual flying hours, we are however taking action, as announced by the Defence Secretary in March 2007, to increase our battlefield helicopter fleet and improve the flexibility we are able to offer operational commanders. These measures include: the acquisition of six Merlin aircraft (previously delivered to Denmark but never used operationally) which will be available within a year; and the conversion of eight existing Chinook Mark 3 helicopters to make them available for deployment in two years. We also continue to refine future acquisition plans to ensure we maximise the military capability we can get from available funding and build a balanced helicopter fleet to meet future requirements.

Work also continues to explore ways of further exploiting all helicopter fleets to provide more operational flying hours. An ongoing programme of logistics transformation is already delivering a range of benefits. These arrangements (so called Integrated Operational Support (IOS) programmes) are based on long-term partnering with industry and already exist on Chinook and Merlin. Similar arrangements for Sea King, Apache and Puma are under development.

[2] Other parameters used: operational serviceability, size of Forward Fleet, number of helicopters "fit for purpose".
[3] The structural integrity of airframes is monitored during service and the life of the platform reviewed on the findings.
[4] The most cost-effective way to do this is to equip helicopters with just the fixed fittings for a capability, thus allowing the more expensive avionics Line Replacement Units to be moved between helicopters.

The level of helicopter activity demanded in-theatre is established by the operational planning process.[5] This is conducted by PJHQ and the Theatre Commander in full recognition of the realities of crew and helicopter availability, the capacity of the logistic infrastructure, and the impacts on long-term sustainability. The continuing high demand on our helicopter capability is fully recognised. As a high priority we are taking steps to improve the number of flying hours we are able to offer Theatre Commanders.

We recognise that the high tempo of operations and associated level of flying hours has led to increased pressures on crew, for example in the number and frequency of tours that some individuals have been asked to undertake. The achievement of aircrew harmony however varies between platform types. The welfare of our personnel is of the utmost importance and is closely monitored. Deployed flying personnel are well trained for the environments in which they operate, including for the frequently hostile combat conditions encountered. When requirements dictate the deployment of higher numbers of personnel, it is in the interest of Flight Safety, but may be contrary to harmony guidelines. We constantly review the number of deployed personnel in an attempt to recover harmony guidelines

A note outlining the feasibility of installing air conditioning in Warrior armoured vehicles and other vehicles in theatre, and an assessment of the trade-off between the amount of money which could be spent on installing air conditioning and the cost of evacuating people because of heat related casualties. (Q 184)

We now have an extensive programme to fit air conditioning units to many of our current and future armoured fighting vehicles and protected patrol vehicles. For example, Challenger Main Battle Tanks, CVR(T), Bulldog, Mastiff and Vector vehicles have environmental control units (ECU—air conditioning) fitted.

Air conditioning is already provided for Warrior drivers and as part of the extensive programme to fit air conditioning units to vehicles, Warrior vehicle crew compartments will be provided with ECU systems to afford cooler operating temperatures for the occupants and vehicle systems. Prototype trials demonstrated the feasibility of the system and a significant reduction in crew compartment temperature was achieved. New Warrior ECU systems have been delivered to Iraq, although technical difficulties have been encountered. A modification kit is currently being delivered in order to resolve the remaining technical issues. All Warrior vehicles deployed to Afghanistan will be fitted with fully modified ECUs and initial feedback from the user has been very positive. Specialist Warrior variants already have ECUs fitted.

ECUs are currently being delivered and fitted to a majority of our logistic vehicles including DROPs vehicles and Heavy Equipment Transporters (the Close Support Tanker already has a system fitted).

In addition to the extensive programme to fit air conditioning to vehicles, we have examined other methods of combating high temperatures and mitigating the effects of excessive heat. Access to cold drinking water will be provided to soldiers operating from Warrior vehicles and we are also investigating the use of reflective blankets on the top of vehicles to reflect solar heat. Pragmatic measures like keeping vehicles in shade with hatches closed during the hottest time of day are also applied when and where practical.

Any reduction in heat casualties as a result of expenditure on the provision of air conditioning for vehicles would not automatically lead to a commensurate reduction in the cost of casualty evacuation. The requirement for a comprehensive casualty evacuation (and AEROMED evacuation) system will be enduring, for broader operational requirements.

An explanation of how the Department defines the task of "over watch" for UK Armed Forces in MND(SE), including details of whether effective over watch could it be achieved from outside Iraq?

Overwatch is a term specific to UK forces within Multi-National Division (South-East (MND(SE)) and is used to describe the force posture for a given province. It is sub-divided into three phases: Tactical, Operational and Strategic.

TACTICAL OVERWATCH

When a province is this phase, UK forces are responsible for security. Initially, they are responsible for the routine provision of security. Over time, routine and non-essential Multi-National Force (MNF) activity progressively reduces, as Iraqi Security Forces (ISF) take increasing responsibility for providing security as a means of moving towards security self-reliance.

---

[5] The Command Estimate is the process used.

OPERATIONAL OVERWATCH

In the Operational Overwatch phase, the province has transferred to Iraqi control and the ISF have responsibility for security. MNF provide a re-intervention capability, but the requirement to intervene will be only *in extremis* and at the request of the Iraqi authorities. The main effort for MND(SE) during this phase is Security Sector Reform, through continued mentoring and training of the ISF, in particular the Iraqi Army. In addition, however, MND(SE) is also required to carry out a number of designated Coalition tasks such as protection of supply routes and points of entry.

The Operational Overwatch phase is the point at which a province is first described publicly as being in a state of "overwatch", hence Al Muthanna, Dhi Qar and Maysan provinces are at the Operational Overwatch stage.

STRATEGIC OVERWATCH

Current coalition planning envisages a final phase of Strategic overwatch during which the coalition's effort will move to supporting the Iraqi Government and Security Forces in facing strategic threats to their internal and external security.

A note outlining the criteria for assessing readiness for transition to Provincial Iraqi Control

Since April 2006, each Iraqi province has been subjected to comprehensive assessments of its readiness to be handed over to Iraqi responsibility, with a working group considering the readiness for handover and making recommendations accordingly to the Iraqi PM and Coalition commanders.

For security responsibility to transfer from the Multi-National Forces (MNF) to provincial Iraqi control (PIC), however, individual provinces must satisfy four main criteria of conditions:

— Threat assessment—the security conditions and level of threat in the province;

— Iraqi Security Forces (ISF)—their ability to handle the security situation;

— Governance—the capacity of the provincial authorities to manage and be responsible for the security environment; and

— Multi-National Forces (MNF) support—their ability to provide assistance to the ISF should it be needed.

The transfer of responsibility will occur in different provinces at different times according to when the conditions are right to do so.

The process of deciding whether individual provinces are ready for PIC is conducted jointly between MNF and the Iraqi authorities. Each month, Divisional Commanders make an assessment and recommendation against the conditions criteria jointly with the relevant Provincial Governor. In terms of the UK's area of responsibility in Multinational Division (South East), having already handed over security responsibility to Iraqi control in three of its four provinces, the UK Commander completes this process for Basra, the province still to achieve PIC.

Divisional recommendations are sent to Baghdad for review by the US Corps Commander who, in turn, forwards a recommendation to the Iraqi/MNF Joint Committee for the Transfer of Security Responsibility. If the Committee concludes that a province is ready for PIC, then a recommendation is made to the joint Iraqi/MNF Ministerial Committee for National Security where the Iraqi Prime Minister has ultimate responsibility for the final decision.

A note outlining the conditions by which the capacity and readiness of the Iraqi Security Forces is assessed

The coalition strategy in Iraq is to help develop a functioning state. Part of this process involves building and strengthening the Iraqi Security Forces (ISF)—which consists of the Army, Police Service and other security institutions—so that they can take over responsibility for delivering security for the Iraqi people.

This strategy has seen the Iraqis taking direct control over their own security institutions. The Iraqi Police has been under Iraqi control since 2004. The Iraqi Army has progressively been transferred from Multinational Forces (MNF) to Iraqi control, as each Division was trained and equipped and their capacity to cope with the security requirement built. Their evolution takes the route of:

— ISF units are formed while MNF lead security operations;

— ISF units support MNF led security operations;

— ISF lead security operations with MNF support; and

— ISF capable of conducting independent security operations.

This has seen the original 10 Divisions established for the Army now having transferred to the Iraqi Ground Forces Command.

A note outlining the formation of the Iraqi Army 14th Division, including details of when the Department anticipates the 14th Division to deploy

The formation of the 14th Division Iraqi Army (IA) is a Government of Iraq (GoI) initiative in recognition of the 10th IA Division's considerable area of operation, which spans the four south-eastern provinces of Muthanna, Dhi Qar, Maysan and Basra. It is being generated from the existing units of 10th IA Division as well as elements of other units from within the IA, all of which have been trained and equipped over the past three years by the Multi-National Force (MNF). The intention is for the new 14th IA Division to take over from 10th IA Division in Basra.

As an Iraqi initiative, 14th IA Division aims to build upon the experience gained by the 10th Division and is now being formed, trained and equipped by the Iraqi Ground Force Command (IGFC). 14th IA Division currently resides under the authority of General Mohan (4* Iraqi Army), head of the Basra Operations Command. The appointment of the General Officer Commanding (GOC) and confirmation of Initial Operation Capability (IOC) is currently planned for November 2007. It will be based in Basra. The UK intends to act as mentor to the 14th IA Division.

10 September 2007

Memorandum from the Redress Trust

INTRODUCTION

1. The Redress Trust (REDRESS) is an international non-governmental organisation with a mandate to ensure respect for the principle that survivors of torture and other cruel, inhuman or degrading treatment and punishment, and their family members, have access to adequate and effective remedies and reparation for their suffering.

2. We are concerned about detention and internment by UK forces in Iraq. We respectfully invite the Committee to use the oral evidence session on "Operations in Iraq" on 24 July as an opportunity to raise a number of concerns regarding the treatment of detainees in UK detention facilities that emerged during the court martial *R v Payne & Others*.

3. We believe that the Minister for the Armed Forces needs to deal with these issues regarding detention and internment in Iraq, and we feel it would be useful for the Committee to investigate whether the concerns of various members of the militarily expressed during the court martial have now been addressed. It would also be an opportunity for the Committee to ask the Minister whether he agrees with former Attorney General Lord Goldsmith QC that there should be an inquiry in to how the army came to authorise particular conditioning techniques.[6]

4. These concerns are based mainly on evidence from some key dates in the court martial transcript, and not a full reading of the whole record. In the limited time available it is not possible to deal with everything arising from the transcript which is a lengthy document. We respectfully suggest that the Committee could possibly make further use of the transcript to raise more questions.

DETENTION AT THE BATTLE GROUP LEVEL

5. One of the developments which led to abuse in Iraq during the Occupation was a shift in policy from transferring detainees to a central facility for holding and questioning within a matter of hours to one allowing Battle Groups to detain and question their own detainees for a number of days. The period between capture and delivery to a central detention facility was a known "danger point" where abuse could occur.[7] Indeed much of the previous abuse, including the tragic death of Baha Mousa, took place at the Battle Group level.

6. Given this, and noting the Memorandum from the Ministry of Defence sent to the Committee,[8] we welcome the move of internees to the more permanent Divisional Internment Facility (DIF) at Basra Air Station. This move may have already taken place. However, if not, we feel it important for the Minister to assure the Committee that the new facility will be operational before the temporary facility at Shaibah Logistic Base is closed (otherwise the current internees there might be dispersed back to Battle Group or some other "lower" level), and that in any event the length of time in custody at the Battle Group level will not increase.

---

[6] "We need to understand why anybody thought, if they did—and somebody obviously did—that these were permissible techniques to be used. I think that is something which needs to be inquired into." Lord Goldsmith giving oral evidence to the Joint Committee on Human Rights, 26 June 2007, Q196, http://www.publications.parliament.uk/pa/jt200607/jtselect/jtrights/uc394-iii/uc39402.htm

[7] *R v Payne* Court Martial transcript, 8 December 2006 pg 63–64.

[8] http://www.publications.parliament.uk/pa/cm200607/cmselect/cmdfence/209/7011108.htm

7. A further issue arising in the court martial was American reluctance to take in internees at British run facilities (at which the Americans nevertheless strongly influenced policy) during the night, and as a result detainees had to be held over night at the Battle Group level and for longer than had been recommended.[9] The Committee should seek assurances that this is not the case with regard to the temporary facility at Shaibah Logistics Base and that it will not occur or is not occurring at the new dedicated DIF at Basra Air Station.

8. Given the history of poor procedures and treatment at the Battle Group level the Committee should inquire into the current procedures for holding and questioning detainees at the Battle Group level. Issues that should be raised include the procedures for documenting the treatment of detainees, whether a dedicated[10] guard detail and rota is in place to ensure accountability,[11] and the training given to regimental medical staff regarding the reporting of possible detainee abuse.[12]

"CONDITIONING"

9. The court martial heard evidence that it was standard procedure of the Intelligence Corps to use conditioning techniques[13] that the Government gave assurances in 1972 to the House of Commons would no longer be used.[14] We feel it is important that the Committee ask the Minister to investigate the implementation of the 1972 ban and how these techniques came to be used in Iraq despite the ban, and despite the 1978 ruling of the European Court of Human Rights that the techniques constituted inhuman and degrading treatment.[15] In our view this is a fundamental issue of Ministerial responsibility given the history of the ban.[16]

10. The court martial also showed gaps in doctrine on the subject of prisoner of war and civilian detainee and internee handling.[17] It has been somewhat addressed by new advice contained in four Joint Doctrine Publications (JDPs)[18] on the subject. However, the extent to which this has been implemented in practice remains unclear. The Committee should pursue the extent to which the new doctrine is actually used in practice.

TRAINING

11. One of the main issues with regard to conditioning was a lack of Tactical Questioners with up-to-date training. The Committee should seek to find out whether adequate Tactical Questioners and interrogators are now deployable. Further, the Committee should question the Minister as to what conditioning techniques are still used in Iraq, which ones are still taught, and whether in refresher courses it is taught that some previously used techniques are illegal.[19]

Safeguards

12. JDP 10-1 now advises that medical officers are not to state "that a subject meets a specific mental or physical standard for interrogation,"[20] for ethical reasons. We are concerned that the medical examination prior to questioning may have been removed. We invite the Committee to seek clarification from the Minister of the precise role of medical staff before, during and after questioning.

SUMMARISED QUESTIONS

— What is the expected time frame that units are to place detainees in the custody of the Divisional Temporary Detention Facility and/or the Divisional Internment Facility?

— To what extent are detainees held by Units (Battle Groups)?

— Will this change with or during the move to the Divisional Internment Facility?

— Is the Divisional Temporary Detention Facility and will the Divisional Internment Facility be run by the UK or the US, and to what extent?

---

[9] Transcript, 8 December 2006, pg 43.

[10] Transcript, 11 December 2006, pg 78–79, and

[11] Transcript, 22 November 2006, pg 18, also 13 December 2006 pg 33–34.

[12] Transcript, 11 December 2006, pg 12–16.

[13] Transcript, 8 December 2006, pg 12.

[14] *Hansard*, col 744, 2 March 1972, referring to the Parker Committee report.

[15] *Ireland v United Kingdom*, 1976 Year Book on the European Convention on Human Rights 512, 748, 788–94.

[16] Report of the Committee of Privy Counsellors appointed to consider authorised procedures for the interrogation of person suspected of terrorism. (Parker Report) March 1972 Cmd 4901 majority report § 37.

[17] Transcript, 13 December 2006 pg 130, see also pg 96 on lack of policy regarding involvement with US questioners.

[18] JDP 10-1 2006, JDP 10-1.1 2006, JDP 10-1.2 2006 and JDP 10-1.3 2006, available at http://www.mod.uk/DefenceInternet/AboutDefence/CorporatePublications/DoctrineOperationsandDiplomacyPublications/JDP/

[19] It has been stated that "wall standing" and the "Ski Sit" positions are not stress positions but are used in conditioning, see transcript 14 December 2006 pp 41–42 and 67. Clearly the length of time in any one position is determinative of the stress it causes.

[20] JDP 10-1, page 5D-3 (70 in the PDF document)

—   Will it take in detainee/internees 24 hours a day?

—   What procedures are in place to ensure that Human Rights Act is applied at these facilities?

—   Since the Ministry of Defence conceded in the *Al Skeini* that the Human Right Act applies to UK detention facilities in Iraq during, and of course the House of Lords judgement itself, have any procedures or conditions of detention changed, and if so, how?

—   Has the document JDN 3/05 *Tactical Questioning, Debriefing and Interrogation* or other documents been modified to reflect the applicability of the Human Rights Act to detention facilities abroad?

—   Has the Ministry of Defence any plans to make the internal reviews and investigations into detainee abuse available to the Committee for scrutiny?

—   Are procedures now in place to ensure that important procedures and orders are not lost when Units are replaced?

—   To what extent do detainees go though a medical examination before undergoing questioning?

18 July 2007

Memorandum from Dr Eric Herring

EXECUTIVE SUMMARY

In nearly all of the provinces which have been under formal British control, there is clear overall support for the invasion. However, most of the population expect security to improve following a withdrawal of Coalition forces and most think that the US military surge begun in January 2007 has made security worse. The UK has sought to play three roles in relation to Iraq—persuading the US of its views, acting as a broker between the US and other international actors and implementing its own policies independently of the US in southern Iraq—but has failed in all three. With the US making all the key decisions on the state building project, UK armed forces have engaged in what could only be intermittent and intermittently productive operations. In specific times and places, UK forces will carry out positive security tasks for the local population. However, this is insufficient reason for them to remain when the population mostly think they are making the situation worse and want them to leave.

The UK should not support US efforts to strengthen the existing Iraqi Government by armed force and training of security force. As Iraq has no coherent government, and as the lines between the state, insurgents, militias and mafias are blurred, there can be no confidence that training of Iraqi security forces is actually a contribution to strengthening the state. It is just as likely—indeed, often more likely—to result in the strengthening groups which will pursue their own interests, stand in the way of strengthening the Iraqi state and turn on Coalition forces when it suits them. The UK should not support the ethno-sectarian partition of Iraq because it is overwhelmingly opposed by Iraqi public opinion; federalist sentiment in Iraq is divided over the specifics and mostly not ethno-sectarian; and the Iraqi constitution sets out the process of federalisation as one to be decided by Iraqis voting in referenda. Nor should UK forces be kept in Iraq because the US wants them to stay for symbolic purposes or to protect its supply lines. The US role in Iraq is neither legitimate nor prudent and hence not worthy of British support.

Instead, the UK should end its combat role in Iraq. No-one can be sure whether the humanitarian and political situation will become worse or better for Iraqis should Coalition forces leave. But the assessment of most Iraqis is that it would improve, and hence withdrawal would not be "cutting and running"—it would be compliance with clearly expressed Iraqi preferences.

The UK should also promote international and regional diplomacy aimed at making economic, political and non-combat security assistance contingent on acceptance of negotiations and political reconciliation among insurgents, militias and the factions that make up the Iraqi Government.

INTRODUCTION

1. This evidence derives from my academic research on Western policy on Iraq over the last seven years or so based on open source documents and interviews in Iraq (2002), the US and UK. My most recent book *Iraq in Fragments: The Occupation and its Legacy* published in November 2006 by Hurst and Cornell University Press was co-authored with Dr Glen Rangwala (Cambridge): "first-rate . . . a compelling account—the clearest yet available of the 'new Iraq'" (Professor Charles Tripp, author of *A History of Iraq*), "an admirably sober and powerful analysis . . . a must read" (Professor Tareq Ismael, editor *International Journal of Contemporary Iraqi Studies*) and "serious and persuasive . . . Splendidly researched . . . required reading" (Professor Jeffrey Record, USAF Air War College). I was specialist adviser to the Select Committee on Economic Affairs of the House of Lords for its inquiry into economic sanctions in 2006–07. My current research is on the political economy of peacebuilding in Iraq and I recently addressed the Royal United Services Institute in London on British counter-insurgency in Iraq.

WHY THE INVASION WAS WRONG—AND WHY IT HAS MATTERED FOR UK OPERATIONS IN IRAQ

2. Perceptions of illegitimate, illegal and unilateral action matter in terms of undermining the willingness of international actors and the local population to accept the invasion and occupation. The window of opportunity for acceptance of the occupation by much of Iraqi opinion was brief. Only a massively resourced effort which transferred power rapidly to Iraqis would have had any chance of success, and that would have been a huge gamble. Instead, the US embarked on a violent but under-resourced attempt to retain power until the "right" institutions and economy were imposed and until the "right" Iraqis looked like they might be elected. This has been doomed from the outset and has been the essential determinant of the failure of UK operations in Iraq.

3. Did Britain and the US have the legal right to do what they did? No. The invasion was not and would not have been authorised by the UN under international law. That is why they did not go back to the Security Council for a resolution authorising war, having ensured the passage of earlier resolutions by insisting that the US and UK would not treat them as authorisations for war.[21]

4. Did Britain and the US have the moral right to do what they did? No. First, this was a war launched with a mixture of deception and self-deception. If a society is to go to war democratically it must at least be on the basis of the facts presented and debated honestly and accurately. Second, starting a war has potentially huge and potentially uncontrollable consequences—the first of these creates an obligation to prepare for the aftermath (an obligation not taken seriously) and the second creates a presumption against gambling with lives and property through war, requiring compelling evidence of necessity (another obligation not met).

5. The US and British Governments have been propagating the myth that the invasion was based on an intelligence failure—that the expectation was that WMD would be found after the invasion. Some of those who favoured the invasion were persuaded themselves that WMD would be found, but this self-deception was despite, not because of, the intelligence. For example, Carne Ross, who was the First Secretary in charge of Iraq policy at the UK Mission to the UN between 1997 and mid-2002, has said regarding that period:

> It was emphatically our view, and that was based on very careful consideration of the intelligence evidence and the evidence that was gained from inspectors in UNSCOM and later UNMOVIC, that Iraq was not in any substantial way rearming with its weapons of mass destruction . . .[22]

Others such as Scott Ritter, chief UN weapons inspector between 1991 and 1998, made that point repeatedly and publicly before the invasion. It is easy to forget now that there were no finds of WMD or WMD production programmes in Iraq from 1992 onwards because the Iraqis had destroyed them in 1991 and possibly also early 1992.

6. The best and most common defence of the invasion is that getting rid of Saddam Hussein's regime (and economic sanctions) made the current mess worthwhile on balance. However, while a majority of Iraqis polled used to be in favour of the invasion, Iraqi majority opinion is now against the invasion, and increasingly strongly so. In the BBC poll in March 2007, 47% of Iraqis said the invasion was right and 53% said it was wrong.[23] In the BBC's August 2007 poll, 37% said it was right (12% absolutely right) and 63% said it was wrong (35% absolutely wrong).[24] Furthermore, it is no coincidence that those areas which were not actually invaded and occupied (the mainly Kurdish north east) have been most in favour of the occupation, while those areas which have suffered the brunt of US use of force (the mainly Sunni Arab centre) have been most opposed to it. And the around two million who have fled the country as refugees, the further two million displaced and of course the hundreds of thousands of dead will not have featured in the polls. When these factors are taken into consideration, even these negative polls must be regarded as flattering to the occupation.

7. The most damning aspect of the polls for the occupiers is that, among those in the sector of the population—the Sunni Arab one—that has experienced the occupation most directly, opposition has been consistent and almost total. For example, in the August 2007 BBC poll, 97% of Sunni Arabs thought the invasion was wrong (70% absolutely wrong), 93% thought attacks on Coalition forces were acceptable, 95% thought Coalition forces were making security worse and 72% wanted them to leave now. These figures refute the Coalition claim that it is protecting Sunni Arab Iraqis from terrorists. Instead, according to the population, the US is illegitimately imposing its presence.

8. UK forces currently remain in Basra at the airport. They have withdrawn from their bases in Muthanna, Dhi Qar and Maysan provinces but were engaged in combat as recently as June 2007 in the vicinity of Amarah, the capital of Maysan, which resulted in over 100 Iraqi deaths. In nearly all of the provinces which have been under formal British control, there is clear overall support for the invasion. In the ORB poll in February 2007, 70%, 90%, 90% and 49% respectively by province thought themselves better

[21] See http://www.impeachblair.org/ and especially the report
http://www.impeachblair.org/downloads/A_Case_ To_Answer.pdf

[22] Oral evidence of 11 July 2006 to the House of Lords Select Committee on Economic Affairs as part of its inquiry *The Impact of Economic Sanctions, Vol II: Evidence*, p 48. See also his book *Independent Diplomat* (Ithaca: Cornell University Press, 2007), http://www.independentdiplomat.com/html/media.html and especially "War Stories" on that site.

[23] http://news.bbc.co.uk/2/hi/middle_east/6451841.stm

[24] http://news.bbc.co.uk/1/hi/world/middle_east/6983841.stm and
http://news.bbc.co.uk/1/shared/bsp/hi/pdfs/10_09_07_ iraqpoll.pdf

off now, almost no-one thought themselves better off under the previous regime, while 22%, 4%, 5% and 39% thought the two were as bad as each other. However, most of the population expect security to improve following a withdrawal of Coalition forces (60%, 74%, 70%, and 91%). In Basra, 40% expect security to get a great deal better following the withdrawal of Coalition forces and only 5% think it will get a great deal worse. While polling did not generally distinguish between British and US forces, in a Ministry of Defence poll in August 2005, support for attacks on Coalition forces was 25% in Basra and 65% in Maysan province.[25]

9. It is not the case that support for attacks on Coalition forces is restricted to Sunni Arabs. Many Shi'a think that such attacks are acceptable (eg 61% in September 2006 and 50% in August 2007) and even around 15% of Kurds supported them in September 2006.[26]

10. Iraqis have been divided on whether Coalition forces should leave immediately, when security is restored or when Iraqi security forces are stronger. However, the preference for immediate withdrawal has climbed steadily to 47% in August 2007, and there was majority opinion poll support in 2006 among Kurds and Shi'a as well as Sunni Arabs for withdrawal after six months to two years. As far as most Iraqis are concerned, the US military surge begun in January 2007 has made security worse. 72% (more than ever) in August 2007 thought Coalition forces were making security worse, and 61% thought security had become worse in the country as a whole in the preceding six months.

11. It is true that the Iraqi Government wishes Coalition forces to stay, but that government only survives because of those forces, and its legitimacy is overwhelmingly rejected by the mainly Sunni Arab areas in particular that are on the receiving end of the use of force by the United States. The Iraqi Government is elected, but a dictatorship of the majority is counter to the principles of liberal democracy which require that the interests and views of minorities are taken into account. The Sunni Arab population tried boycott and then voting to have its voice heard, and neither worked. Not surprisingly, 86% of Sunni Arabs polled in September 2006 said that they regarded the current Iraqi Government as illegitimate.

12. Brig Gavin Bulloch, retired is currently rewriting UK counter-insurgency doctrine for publication at the end of 2007. In a presentation on 21 September 2007 to a conference held in the Royal United Services Institute, Brig. Bulloch announced that the new doctrine would for the first time include the notion of popular consent as a requirement. This is a development to be welcomed. It contrasts strongly with US Army counter-guerilla doctrine adopted in 2004, which states:

> Commanders must be prepared to operate in a broad range of political atmospheres. The host country's form of government may be anything from an absolute, and not too benevolent, dictatorship to a democracy struggling to establish itself, or anything in between. . . . No matter what political atmosphere prevails in the host country, the brigade commander must engage the guerrilla with every asset at the commander's disposal. He must realize that democratic principles may not be immediately applicable. However, he should act within the limits of his authority to improve the circumstances of the government he was sent to support.[27]

British doctrine is, fortunately, moving in a direction that is incompatible with this US requirement.

UK operations in Iraq have been undermined fatally at the political-strategic level.

13. Counter-insurgency doctrine and practice have two elements—legitimation and coercion. Legitimation is often termed "hearts and minds", and the latter has a practical function (providing guidance on what to do), an ideological function (obscuring counter-insurgency's coercive dark side in which a polity is being imposed violently on an unwilling population) and a self-deceiving function (reassuring those engaged in coercion that they are legitimate because what they would 'really' prefer to do is win hearts and minds but are being forced by their opponents to act coercively).

14. Despite the widespread approbation in Western policy circles at the end of 2006 regarding the appointment of counter-insurgency expert Gen. David Petraeus to lead Coalition forces and the adoption by the US military of its new counter-insurgency doctrine, the US strategy since the beginning of the surge has been based primarily on coercion—for example, aerial bombardment and detention have been at record levels. Subjecting around 25,000 to internment with entirely inadequate due process is wrong and will have the net effect of deepening the Coalition's unpopularity.[28] The same can be said of US air strikes which receive little attention outside Iraq. In the first half of 2007, the US Air Force dropped 437 bombs and missiles in Iraq, triple what it dropped in the second half of 2006 and five times the total for the first half of 2006.[29]

---

[25] Sean Rayment, *Secret MoD Poll: Iraqis Support Attacks on British Troops, Daily Telegraph*, 22 October 2005.

[26] The September 2006 poll is here: http://www.worldpublicopinion.org/pipa/articles/home_page/250.php?nid=&id=&pnt=250&lb=hmpg1

[27] Department of the Army, *US Army Counterguerrilla Operations Handbook*, Guilford (CT: Lyons Press, 2004) pp 1(1), 3(6).

[28] A defence of this policy by the Commander of US detention facilities in Iraq is here: "Bloggers' Roundtable With General Douglas M Stone", *Washington Post*, 18 September 2007.

[29] Charles J Hanley, *Air Force Quietly Building Iraq Presence*, Associated Press, 14 July 2007. http://www.truthout.org/docs_2006/071507Y.shtml

15. The US state building project has lurched repeatedly in different directions, and British political and military operations in Iraq have been deeply affected by those lurches. The original US intention was rapid elections so that Iraqis would install pro-US exiles who would inherit functioning governmental institutions. When the exiles proved incapable and unpopular and governmental institutions collapsed or were abolished by the US, the new model was direct US rule for as long as it took to install an ideal neoconservative state. When that dream evaporated, the US sought rapid formal handover to the alliance of Kurdish paramilitary leaders and Shi'a fundamentalists who dominated the elections. And now the US is floundering in its efforts to bring about some kind of compromise that will incorporate Sunni Arabs and protect what it sees as US strategic interests.

16. The UK has sought to play three roles in relation to Iraq—persuading the US of its views, acting as a broker between the US and other international actors and implementing its own policies independently of the US in southern Iraq—but has failed in all three.[30] With the US making all the key decisions on the state building project, UK armed forces have engaged in what could only be intermittent and intermittently productive operations. The UK military presence in Iraq has been tiny and under-resourced, and the UK political mission in Iraq to which it is meant to be subordinated has been even tinier. There has also been persistent incoherence and lack of integration, with little guidance from London or Baghdad or even neighbouring provinces. In continual fear of being over-run, the priority has been to avoid antagonising excessively existing or rising armed local political actors. UK forces have made reconstruction, anti-militia and anti-corruption efforts such as Operation Sinbad which ran from late 2006 to early 2007. However, this should not obscure the fact that they have tended to be (often uncomprehending) spectators, occasional protagonists and only rarely the centre of power and legitimacy. Their position was notably jeopardised by the ill-conceived and half-hearted US actions such as its offensive against the Mahdi Army in the Spring of 2004.

17. Counter-insurgency usually implies a coherent state that is being protected from overthrow by a clearly separate armed group. In the case of Iraq, the line between the state, insurgents, militias and mafias is blurred. Iraq is a fragmented state in the sense of there being no agreed overall political authority and no means of resolving disputes over its location. There is fragmentation between and within regions, classes, religious sects, ethnicities, government ministries, tribes and political parties. Ethno-sectarian fragmentation into Kurds, Shi'a and Sunni Arabs is only one axis of fragmentation and often not the most important one. The Iraqi Government will not move decisively against militias in general because it is largely rooted in them. The Iraqi Government is not a coherent actor and the line between it and those it is supposedly fighting is blurred, with (for example) Sadrists in and out of government posts. This is even more the case with the state as a whole, most obviously in the case of the security forces which are permeated with embedded insurgents—people taking the pay, training, intelligence and resources of the state security forces but using them against the Coalition and the Iraqi state. It is also the case with supposedly Iraqi but actually almost purely Kurdish or Shi'a Arab units deployed in Sunni Arab areas. This practice generates and exacerbates ethno-sectarian tensions rather than protects Iraqis from insurgents and militias. It seems that a significant proportion of Kurdish troops speak little or even no Arabic, which can only contribute to inter-communal alienation.

WHAT'S LEFT FOR THE UK TO DO IN IRAQ?

18. The UK should not support US efforts to strengthen the existing Iraqi Government by armed force and training of security forces, and should not support ethno-sectarian partition. Nor should UK forces be kept in Iraq because the US wants them to stay for symbolic purposes or to protect its supply lines. Instead, the UK should promote international and regional diplomacy aimed at making economic, political and non-combat security assistance contingent on acceptance of negotiations and political reconciliation among insurgents, militias and the factions that make up the Iraqi Government.[31]

Military backing for the existing Iraqi Government?

19. There has been far too much willingness to accept the US claim that the decline in the number of attacks between late July and mid September represent successes for the surge. First, the level of attacks was at an all time high in May and June, despite the extreme summer heat. Second, other factors were probably more important in the decline in attacks—insurgents resting and regrouping after their surge in attacks, insurgents and militias lying low as the surge passed their areas, unsustainable bans on the use of vehicles in places such as Falluja and parts of Baghdad, segregation through displacement and rumoured Saudi and Jordanian behind the scenes efforts.[32] The US's own figures show that the average daily casualties in Iraq

---

[30] See Glen Rangwala and Eric Herring, *Britain in Iraq: Neither Poodle Nor Partner But Failed Protagonist*, submission to the independent Iraq Commission on the scope and focus of Britain's future involvement in Iraq, 10 June 2007. http://www.channel4.com/news/microsites/I/the_iraq_commission/pdfs/rangwala_herring_submission.pdf

[31] For more on this, see Rangwala and Herring, *Britain in Iraq*.

[32] University of Michigan Middle East scholar Professor Juan Cole has been following these issues with care. See http://www.juancole.com/

remained at near-record levels for the entire period of the surge since February 2007 inclusive, with only a slight dip in June.[33] More importantly, there can be no military victory in Iraq for the Coalition: the key measure of success has to be political progress, and that has not occurred.

20. The US military surge has not achieved its stated goal of creating the space for political reconciliation: instead it has had the opposite effect of removing the political incentive for it. The Kurdish and Shi'a groups favoured by the US in the Iraqi Government have not had to compromise because they have been able to rely on the US military to prop them up.[34]

21. The process of training Iraqi army and especially police forces is suffering from poor retention rates of weapons as well as personnel.[35] But there is an even deeper problem. As the state is fragmented, there can be no confidence that training of Iraqi security forces is actually a contribution to strengthening the state. It is just as likely—indeed, often more likely—to result in the strengthening groups which will pursue their own interests, stand in the way of strengthening the Iraqi state and turn on Coalition forces when it suits them. The problem with Iraqi security forces is not lack of training but alternative loyalties, which is precisely why the US is reluctant to provide them with weapons, especially heavier ones. The Iraqi Government has complained publicly about this, and the US Government, torn between fear of what Iraqis will do with the weapons and the need to arm Iraqi forces to take over from US ones, has recently boosted its arms sales to Iraq.[36] Even if some groups, such as tribal ones, work with Coalition forces, such alignments will be temporary and contingent, and are not evidence of endorsement of the Coalition's goals or presence.

22. Violence in Basra escalated recently and the situation remains unstable.[37] In specific times and places, UK forces will carry out positive security tasks for the local population. However, this is insufficient reason for them to remain when the population mostly think they are making the situation worse and want them to leave.

Support partition?

23. There is much talk, especially in Washington, of backing some form of top-down ethno-sectarian partition, either hard partition (separate states) or soft partition (a federation with a relatively weak centre). The UK should not back schemes for partition in Iraq because they are completely against the wishes of most Iraqis. Federalist sentiment in Iraq is divided over the specifics and mostly not ethno-sectarian and the Iraqi constitution sets out the process of federalisation as a bottom-up process via referenda.[38]

24. In terms of responsibility for most of the violence in Iraq, Iraqis mainly blame the Coalition, followed by al Qaeda/foreign jihadists; and then roughly equal blame for the Iraqi government, Sunni and Shi'a militias and leaders, sectarian disputes, common criminals and Iran. The fact that Iraqis mostly blame non-Iraqis for the violence is indicative of a continuing national sentiment.

25. Kurds are fairly consistently positive about the invasion and the performance of the Coalition politically and militarily. Shi'i tend to be more positive than Sunni Arabs about the invasion but similarly negative about the occupation and Coalition forces. However, it is fundamentally misleading and dangerous to attribute a single view to each supposed ethno-sectarian "group". The notion of "Iraqi" is still of great significance and value, even as ethno-sectarian aspects of identity become more prominent due to a structure of political incentives which rewards ethno-sectarian mobilisation and seems to require it for self-protection. Furthermore, the local or regional is an important level of identity, interests and concerns which may complement or compete with the national and the ethno-sectarian. Opinion polls show that Iraqis overwhelmingly think that separation of people on sectarian lines is a bad thing (98% in August 2007) and that the separation on such lines that has occurred has been forced. Most Iraqis want a unified Iraq with a strong central government in Baghdad (and a substantial minority want regionalised government and a federal government in Baghdad, without suggesting that this is ethno-sectarian).

26. The overall picture is a fairly strong though variable continuing commitment to the idea of an Iraqi nation and to its expression in the form of a self-determining Iraqi state. The weakest commitment is among Kurds, but even there it is too easy to exaggerate the contrasts between Kurdish and Arab Iraqi views. For example, polled in late 2004, more Kurds expressed a preference for living in an ethnically mixed Iraq than for living in an independent Kurdish state. Kurdish political elites assert a Kurdish right to independence but a willingness to live in an autonomous region within a federal Iraq. At both popular and elite levels, desire for an independent state is tempered by an awareness of the risks of pursuing that goal (such as invasion and occupation by Turkey).

---

[33] US Department of Defence (DoD), *Measuring Security and Stability in Iraq*, 14 September 2007, p 20. http://www.defenselink.mil/pubs/pdfs/Signed-Version-070912.pdf

[34] See, for example, Robert H. Reid, *In Iraq, Little Pressure for Reforms*, Associated Press, 12 September 2007.

[35] US DoD, *Measuring Security and Stability*, p 35. Brian Katulis, Lawrence J Korb and Peter Juul, *Strategic Reset: Reclaiming Control of US Security in the Middle East*, June 2007, p 19.

[36] *Iraq Envoy Slams US Over Arms Supplies*, Agence France Presse, 26 July 2007; "US Plans $2.3 bn Arms Sale to Iraq", al-Jazeera.net, 26 September 2007.

[37] Kim Sengupta, "Surge in Basra Killings May Force British Back to City", *The Independent*, 26 September 2007.

[38] For authoritative and extensive exposition of these points, see the work of Dr Reidar Vissser, Research Fellow, Norwegian Institute of International Affairs, at http://www.historiae.org/

Keep UK forces in Iraq to provide symbolic and practical support for the US?

27. Some favour keeping UK forces in Iraq protecting supply lines or so that the US Government is not displeased at losing its main symbolic ally. The US is fully capable of protecting its own supply lines. More importantly, for the reasons given throughout this evidence, the US role in Iraq is neither legitimate nor prudent and hence not worthy of British support. The Bush administration's bottom line in Iraq appears to be to avoid losing until the United States has a Democrat as president (a real prospect in the November 2008 election), and then blame defeat on the Democrats for their weakness and the Iraqis for their fecklessness and ingratitude. A Labour Government or indeed any British Government should not let British soldiers die for this cause. Supporting US operations in Iraq practically or symbolically would require the UK must also share some responsibility for the US actions in Iraq.

Promote international and regional diplomacy which makes non-combat assistance for factions in Iraq conditional on their commitment to negotiations and political reconciliation

28. No-one can be sure whether the humanitarian and political situation will become worse or better for Iraqis should Coalition forces leave. But the assessment of most Iraqis is that it would improve, and hence withdrawal would not be "cutting and running"—it would be compliance with clearly expressed Iraqi preferences.

29. To a great extent events in Iraq are, and always have been, beyond the control of the US and British governments, and trying to gain it militarily and unilaterally with a coating of superficial multilateralism will continue the march to failure and make it even harder for the situation to be retrieved by anyone (and that will have to be mainly Iraqis). The US and UK governments need a paradigm shift in their approach from control to influence, from violence to non-violence and from unilateralism to multilateralism.[39] This shift might be beyond them, but the imminent prospect of defeat and escalating chaos may push them in that direction. Assistance in training of security forces and economic reconstruction can and should be provided only to the extent that it assists the realisation of the overwhelming Iraqi preference for a democratic and coherent Iraqi state that is not organised around ethno-sectarianism. In effect, this approach takes benchmarks of political progress seriously. The Coalition approach has been to provide support to the existing Iraqi Government as an incentive to make progress. The reverse approach must be adopted, that is, support should be provide as a reward for actual progress. Furthermore, those rewards should be provided to any committed to negotiation and reconciliation.

30. There are many intertwined but also in some respects independent armed conflicts in Iraq in the north-east, the centre, Baghdad and the south. They will end when the key actors (a) think they can gain more from negotiating than fighting (either to continue a stalemate or to achieve victory) and (b) are be able to deliver their constituencies in support of a deal reached through negotiations. In other words, they have to be willing and able to negotiate. At present, neither condition exists and the creation of those conditions is not being prioritised at present by the US and UK. It may be that externally-provided rewards will not be able to make a major difference in bringing about those conditions, but at least the effort would be being made, and without the UK being involved in or supporting illegitimate and counter-productive uses of force and detention.

28 September 2007

Memorandum from the Ministry of Defence

PRE-VISIT BRIEF

Asterisks denote that part of the evidence which, for security reasons, has not been reported at the request of the Ministry of Defence and with the agreement of the Committee.

OPERATIONAL OVERVIEW

1. United Kingdom forces continued their deployment in Iraq under the mandate of United Nations Security Council Resolution (UNSCR) 1723, which provided renewed authority for the Multi-National Force—Iraq (MNF-I) to operate in Iraq until December 2007. The MNF-I is led by the United States and divides Iraq into six sectors of divisional command and control. The UK's area of responsibility covers the Multi-National Division-South East (MND-SE), which incorporates four of Iraq's 18 provinces (Al Muthanna; Maysan; Dhi Qar and Basra). MND-SE is currently commanded by Major General Jonathan Shaw.

---

[39] The work of the Oxford Research Group on the sustainable security paradigm is at the cutting edge. See http://www.oxfordresearchgroup.org.uk

2. As one of 26 nations contributing to MNF-I, UK forces are the second largest contributor of international military assistance behind the United States, with a current force level of around 5,500. The majority of troops are based in MND-SE, although the UK also provides officers to other key coalition appointments, such as the Deputy Commander MNFiI, currently Lieutenant General Graeme Lamb.

3. Five nations are deployed alongside the UK in MND-SE at present—Australia, Czech Republic, Denmark, Lithuania, and Romania. Both Japan and Italy ended their contributions to military ground operations in MND(SE) this year.

4. The 26 nations together contribute approximately 160,000 troops to the MNF-I, with the US the largest contributor with approximately 143,000 troops. Most troop contributing nations are subject to political mandates for their deployments. Individual national mandates are often linked to their support of UNSCR 1723. Details of the troop contributing nations are as follows:

Albania	Armenia	Australia	Azerbaijan
Bosnia-Herzegovina	Bulgaria	Czech Republic	Denmark
El Salvador	Estonia	Georgia	Japan
Kazakhstan	Latvia	Lithuania	Macedonia
Moldova	Mongolia	Poland	Romania
Singapore	Slovakia	South Korea	Ukraine
UK	US		

5. In line with the Prime Minister's February announcement this year, the number of UK forces reduced from around 7,100 to the current level of around 5,500. We are also reposturing our forces, and over the last few months have transferred three fixed bases to the Iraqi Army—The Shatt al Arab Hotel, the Old State Building and the Shaibah Logistics Base. It remains our aim to move all our forces to a single fixed base at Basra Air Station and hand back the Basra Palace site to the Iraqi authorities in late summer, depending on conditions and progress. This re-posturing has helped free up British personnel from force protection and allowed logistical efficiencies, all of which enabling us to concentrate on training and mentoring the ISF.

6. The coalition's aim remains to protect Iraqis and their efforts at building democratic structures, with the priority on enabling the Iraqis to take responsibility for their own security. The three main tasks for coalition forces in MND(SE) are:

— Training and support to the Iraqi Security Forces (ISF).

— Operations in support of the Iraqi Department of Border Enforcement.

— Targeted Strike operations in the pursuit of a secure environment.

7. The lead UK unit in Iraq is 1 Mechanised Brigade, which took over the command of UK forces on 1 June 2007. It s commanded by Brigadier James Bashall. The major units are:

— 1 Mechanised Brigade Headquarters and Signal Squadron (215 Signal Squadron Royal Signals)

— 2 Squadrons from the Household Cavalry Regiment

— The Kings Royal Hussars

— 2 Squadrons from the 2nd Royal Tank Regiment (2RTR)

— 1st Battalion Irish Guards

— 1 Company from the 1st Battalion The Royal Welsh

— 2nd Battalion The Royal Welsh

— 4th Battalion The Rifles

— 1st Regiment Royal Horse Artillery

— 22 Engineer Regiment

— 1 Squadron from 23 Pioneer Regiment Royal Logistic Corps

— 3 Logistic Support Regiment Royal Logistic Corps

— 1 Company from 6 Battalion Royal Electrical & Mechanical Engineers

— Bravo (16) Close Medical Support Squadron,3 Close Support Medical Regiment, Royal Army Medical Corps

— 158 Provost Company3rd Regiment Royal Military Police

— 22 Battery, 32 Regiment Royal Artillery

— 34 Field Hospital Royal Army Medical Corps

SECURITY SITUATION

8. Despite recent tragic events involving the deaths of British forces, and a number of security related incidents across MND(SE), the security situation remains relatively quiet compared to other parts of the country. However, Basra continues to suffer from violence mainly between Shia groups, with the remainder of other attacks aimed at coalition forces in MND(SE).

9. The security situation across the rest of Iraq varies from province to province. In Baghdad and surrounding areas, violence perpetrated by sectarian and insurgent groups remains a very serious problem. Recent action by Iraqi and coalition forces as part of the Baghdad security plan has led to a reduction in murders by the militia death squads. But the terrorist groups continue to use suicide bombings to inflame the sectarian divide, such as the bombing in June of the al-Askari Mosque in Samarra. Outside Baghdad and its environs—which account for around 80% of the violence in Iraq—the security situation is better, particularly in the north and south of the country.

10. The joint coalition/Iraqi Baghdad Security Plan called Operation Fardh al Qanoon, started in February this year with the intention of reducing sectarian violence in the capital and surrounding provinces, in order to create the political breathing space necessary for substantive progress on national reconciliation. While the last of the US surge units have recently arrived in Baghdad and it is still too early to judge the success of the Plan, indications to date show some signs for encouragement. High profile suicide attacks remain of deep concern, while levels of other forms of sectarian violence have decreased and the ISF have so far performed well. The commitment to date shown by the Iraqi authorities in tackling this situation is very welcome. Importantly, PM Maliki has pledged that political or sectarian interference in the plan will not be tolerated. General Petraeus and Ambassador Crocker are due to give their first report to the US authorities on progress with the Operation in September.

FORCE PROTECTION

11. Force protection continues to be a priority. In response to increasing attacks, all aspects of the protection of personnel have been enhanced by continuous improvements in tactics and training, supported by the development of improved body armour, new armoured vehicles [* * * * * *] to reduce the risks to UK personnel. UK forces in MND(SE) have achieved a number of successes against those who seek to target coalition forces, the ISF and Iraqi civilians. As part of this, they have detained individuals, and recovered weapons, ammunition and other material.

POLITICAL PROCESS

12. In political terms, Iraq has come a long way in a very short time. The Iraqi people have shown their passion and commitment to a democratic future after decades of dictatorship by voting in their millions in the first free national elections and on Iraq's constitution. During 2006, in a process backed by the UN, the first fully elected Government of Iraq—the Iraqi National Unity Government—was formed of representatives from across all the main elements of Iraqi society. The Prime Minister—Nouri al Maliki—was nominated on 22 April 2006 and he announced his Government on 20 May 2006. Key appointments are:

— President: Jalal Talabani
— Prime Minister: Nouri Al-Maliki
— Vice Presidents: Dr Tareq Al-Hashimi; Dr Adel Abdul Mehdi
— Deputy Prime Ministers: Dr Salaam Zawba'i; Dr Barham Saleh
— Minister for the Interior: Jawad al-Bolani
— Minister for Defence: General Abdel Qader Jassim
— Minister for National Security: Sherwan al-Waili
— Minister for Foreign Affairs: Hoshyar Zebari
— Minister for Finance: Bayan Jabr
— Minister for Oil: Dr Hussein Shahristani

PM Maliki's government of national unity represents all sectors of the community and it is having to face very difficult problems, not least the security in those provinces and cities plagued by inter-communal and insurgent violence. It has repeatedly reiterated the need to root out sectarianism.

13. It may take many years for a peaceful, democratic Iraq to mature, but we and the international community must stand alongside the Iraq people to help them develop their economy, their infrastructure and democratic institutions.

14. Political progress is continually being demonstrated. Seven of Iraq's eighteen provinces have been handed over to Iraqi control, including three out of the four provinces which make up the UK's area of operations in southern Iraq. These handovers demonstrate Iraq's continuing progress in building up its

political institutions and, in partnership with the Coalition, its security capacity. More provinces are expected to go through this process in the coming months, as conditions permit, including Basra province later in 2007.

TRANSITION

15. The UK is committed to Iraq for as long as the Iraqi Government judge that the coalition is required to provide security and to assist the Iraqi Security Forces. Progress will depend not on reaching certain dates, but on achieving certain conditions which will be based upon principals outlined by the Iraqi Joint Committee to Transfer Security (JCTSR).

16. Since April 2006, each Iraqi province has been subjected to comprehensive assessments of its readiness to be handed over to Iraqi responsibility, with a working group considering the readiness for handover and making recommendations accordingly to the Iraqi PM and Coalition commanders. Assessments are made against four well publicised conditions: the insurgents' threat level; the Iraqi Security Forces' ability to take on the security task; the capacity of provincial bodies to cope with the changed security environment; and the posture and support available from Coalition Forces. The transfer of responsibility will occur in different provinces at different times according to when the conditions are right to do so.

17. The UK plans for southern Iraq are part of, and consistent with, Coalition plans and the Iraqi-led transition process. With our Iraqi and Coalition partners we continue to be involved in the assessment of the criteria for transfer in those provinces for which we have responsibility.

18. Real progress is now being made. Seven of Iraq's 18 provinces have transferred to Iraqi control and more provinces are expected to go through this process in the coming months as conditions permit. This demonstrates Iraq's continuing progress in building up its political institutions and, in partnership with the Coalition, its security capacity. The Iraqi Government's desire to accelerate its assumption of responsibility is very encouraging and, in supporting the Iraqi Government, we are equally keen to progress to the point at which the Iraqis can operate without MNF assistance.

19. Of the seven provinces that have transitioned to date, Al Muthanna and Dhi Qar in the UK's area of operations were the first provinces to transfer to Iraqi control in July and September 2006 respectively. Najaf province in the neighbouring US area of operations followed in December. Maysan province, also in the UK's area of operations, transferred in mid-April 2007. The most recent provinces to transfer to Iraqi control in, May 2007, were three Kurdish provinces—Irbil, Suleymaniyah and Dohuk.

SECURITY SECTOR REFORM

20. The coalition is undertaking one of the most ambitious security sector reform programmes in modern times and has so far trained and equipped over 353,000 members of the Iraqi Security Forces (ISF)—over 194,000 in the Ministry of Interior (including the police) and over 158,000 in the Ministry of Defence (including the Army). Development of the ISF and Security Sector Reform (SSR) is currently overseen by the Multi-national Security Transition Command—Iraq (MNSTC-I), led by Lieutenant General James Dubik. His deputy is the British Brigadier Stephen Gledhill. MOD has overall responsibility for the delivery of Iraqi Security Forces in MND(SE), including the police.

21. The UK is responsible for training and mentoring the 10th Division of the Iraqi Army based in MND(SE). It is commanded by Major General Habib. In January this year, 10 Division transferred from coalition command to the Iraqi Ground Force Command based in Baghdad. Eight of the other Divisions have also transferred, leaving one remaining under coalition command which is due to transfer in the next few months. 10 Division proved its professionalism during Operation SINBAD and is now planning and leading security operations in Basra City with minimal Coalition support. Two 10 Division battalions also performed well in Baghdad supporting Operation Fardh al Qanoon.

22. We are also responsible for training and mentoring the Iraqi Police Service (IPS) in MND(SE). The IPS has made encouraging progress, particularly during Op SINBAD but we and the Iraqis accept that corruption and criminality in the police force remain a problem. We will continue to work with the Iraqi authorities to remove corrupt and inefficient officers, but ultimately only the Iraqi authorities are in a position to effect the required organisational / cultural change. PM Maliki has now appointed a new Provincial Director of Police for Basra, Major General Jalil. On a practical level, and with the assistance of over 50 FCO-led International Police Advisors, the MoD is helping to develop specific niche training programmes in leadership, intelligence and internal affairs that help build long-term capacity.

23. The UK has continued to play a lead role in developing the Iraqi Navy (formerly the Iraqi Coastal Defence Force), providing a team of around 30 UK personnel located at Umm Qasr Naval Base south of Basra to train and mentor Iraqi naval and marine personnel, as well as officer training at Britannia Royal Naval College Dartmouth and HMS Collingwood in the UK. We have also provided seaborne support to the Iraqi Navy and Marines during maritime security operations in the northern Arabian Gulf.

24. Overall, emphasis continues on developing capability rather than numbers, particularly in the key capabilities—leadership, command and control, intelligence, logistics—which will enable the Iraqis to take over control of security themselves. This will take time and effort.

RECONSTRUCTION

25. Twenty years of under-investment and degradation to Iraqi infrastructure will take time to rectify. Reconstruction continues despite security problems and sabotage of power and pipelines. Iraq has a stable economy; more people have access to drinking water and sewerage systems; there has been a decline in malaria, polio, measles, and mumps; independent media is flourishing and some 2,500 NGOs are registered with the Government.

26. The UK has disbursed the £544 million pledged at the Madrid Conference in 2003. Since then, the UK has pledged an additional £200 million, including the £100 million pledged by the Foreign Secretary at the Ministerial launch of the International Compact for Iraq on 3 May 2007. This makes a total UK commitment of £744 million. The funding has contributed to international efforts which have achieved the following:

— Over 5,000 schools rehabilitated and a further 1,000 in progress. More than 100,000 primary and 40,000 secondary teachers trained.

— Over five million children have received life-saving vaccinations.

— 1,000 healthcare facilities have been rehabilitated or equipped and more than 6,000 staff trained.

— 2,500 Iraqi NGOs are now registered with the Iraqi government and trade unions.

— 217 Iraqi judges, 288 lawyers and 71 prosecutors trained in human rights, international humanitarian law, and independence of judiciary.

— Over 3,000 women and young people in the south trained in business skills.

— Over 180 journalists trained in independent journalism and feature writing.

— 250 newspapers and magazines have been launched. New TV and radio stations have been set up.

27. The Iraqi Government has the lead on reconstruction and development in Iraq. New systems for coordinating Iraqi and donor funding are up and running, including Sector Working Groups in rule of law, energy, education, and health. These groups are led by Iraqi Ministries and are responsible for drawing up strategies to support reconstruction in the medium to long term.

28. The Department for International Development (DFID) is leading the UK's reconstruction programme in support of the Iraqi Government's National Development Strategy (NDS). It plays a full role in donor coordination, both inside Iraq through the Baghdad Co-ordination Group, and internationally in the International Reconstruction Fund Facility for Iraq (IRFFI) Donor Committee and other less formal processes. More than $1.3 billion has been paid by donors to IRFFI, consisting of UN and World Bank Trust Funds to support reconstruction in Iraq, with DFID contributing £70 million—£40 million to the World Bank Trust Fund and £30 million to the United Nations Trust Fund.

29. DFID's programme focuses on:

— macro-economic reform—advising the Iraqi Government on essential economic reforms which will unlock billions of dollars of Iraq's revenues to finance their own reconstruction;

— developing effective and accountable institutions at the centre of government and in the south;

— improving power and water supplies in the south and advising the Government on a national power sector strategy; and

— funding grass-roots projects to encourage poor and vulnerable people to participate in the political process.

SECURITY INTERNMENT IN IRAQ

30. UNSCR 1723 is the authority under which MNF-I commanders are able to intern individuals in Iraq for imperative reasons of security, as a means of protecting both their own forces and the Iraqi people. Internment is a critical component of our approach to ensuring the security and stability of Iraq, and to force protection.

31. The UK uses this power sparingly: we currently have 100 internees in the new purpose-built Divisional Internment Facility (DIF) at the Contingency Operating Base in Basra, which opened earlier this year. The number of internees held changes frequently, but is published on the MOD website and updated monthly. There are written orders covering all aspects of the running of the DIF, and UK internment is monitored by the International Committee of the Red Cross (ICRC). Relations with the ICRC are good, and they intend to make their first visit to the new facility in the coming weeks. The Iraqi Minister of Human Rights has also requested to visit the facility in the near future.

32. Our policy is to hold only those deemed an imperative threat to security, in accordance with UNSCR 1723 which continues the powers that were set out in UNSCR 1546 (and the letters from former Prime Minister Allawi and former US Secretary of State Powell annexed thereto).

33. There is a structured review process in theatre for all UK internees. Individuals held by the UK have their cases reviewed on a monthly basis by the Divisional Internment Review Committee (a UK committee comprising Military and Civilian personnel). Individuals no longer considered to be a threat are released. There is also a review process with Iraqi involvement on a less frequent basis.

34. We transfer internees into the Iraqi criminal justice system where there is a sufficiently strong evidential case. To date five cases have concluded, with four acquittals and one conviction. [*   *   *   *   *   *   *] Court liaison personnel monitor progress on the cases of criminal detainees we have transferred to the Central Criminal Court Iraq.

IRAN

35. Foreign forces in Iraq and Afghanistan continue to be a source of concern to Tehran. The leadership believes that US and UK forces in particular are part of a wider plan to encircle and intimidate Iran; ultimately Tehran fears that the presence of coalition and ISAF forces on its borders could be used as a springboard for regime change.

36. We know that support from within Iran goes to groups who are attacking our forces, and consider that any Iranian links to armed groups in Iraq outside the political process, either through supply of weapons, training or funding, are unacceptable. In our assessment, some of the Improvised Explosive Devices that are being used against our troops use technology that originates from Iran.

37. The UK continues to press Iran to cut its links with armed groups operating in Iraq, and to do more to improve border security and fight terrorism. The Iranians are well aware of our concerns about this, as Ministers and officials have raised Iranian interference in Iraq with the Iranian authorities on many occasions over the last year. We are also, through the Iraqi Government and their engagement with the Iranian Government, aiming to send the strong message that it is not in Iran's interests to have a destabilised southern Iraq. On a practical level, UK forces are continuing their training and mentoring of the Iraqi Department of Border Enforcement (DBE), which has ultimate responsibility for border issues.

2 July 2007

Printed in the United Kingdom by The Stationery Office Limited
12/2007   381877   19585

ISBN 978-0-215-03759-6

9 780215 037596